MW00588602

ECLIPSE AND RE-EMERGENCE OF THE COMMUNIST MOVEMENT

Revolutionary Pocketbooks

Eclipse and Re-emergence of the Communist Movement
Gilles Dauvé and François Martin

Voices of the Paris Commune
edited by Mitchell Abidor

From Crisis to Communisation
Gilles Dauvé

Death to Bourgeois Society: The Propagandists of the Deed
edited by Mitchell Abidor

ECLIPSE AND RE-EMERGENCE OF THE COMMUNIST MOVEMENT

Gilles Dauvé and François Martin

Eclipse and Re-emergence of the Communist Movement
Gilles Dauvé and François Martin
This edition copyright © 2015 PM Press

All rights reserved. No part of this book may be transmitted by any
means without permission in writing from the publisher.

ISBN: 978–1–62963–043–4

Library of Congress Control Number: 2014908066

Cover by John Yates/Stealworks
Interior design by briandesign

10 9 8 7 6 5 4 3 2 1

PM Press
PO Box 23912
Oakland, CA 94623
www.pmpress.org

Printed in the USA by the Employee Owners of Thomson-Shore in
Dexter, Michigan. www.thomsonshore.com

Note: Half of the texts in the present book were written and made public in France between 1969 and 1972. This anthology is published for the third time (or the fourth including a partial Japanese edition). Instead of adding yet another preface, the editors thought it better to end the book with a "postlude" in order to take stock of how times have changed since the 1970s.

In this PM Press edition, extensive changes have been made in chapters 1, 2, 3, and 4. Chapters 5 and 6 are new, and so is chapter 7, the postlude.

■ CONTENTS

■ PREFACE TO THE JAPANESE EDITION OF NO. 1 AND NO. 2 OF *LE MOUVEMENT COMMUNISTE*

The first two essays in this book were translated and published in Japan in the 1970s. Here is the 1973 preface, modified and abridged with new notes added.[1]

In France, as everywhere else, what is usually known as Marxism has nothing to do with revolution. In this topsy-turvy world, wage-labourers are exploited in "socialist" countries, while "communist parties" support capitalism in more ways than one. Communism has become a synonym for working hard and obeying one's "socialist" boss. Most parties called communist have been and are nationalist, colonialist, and imperialist. As Paul Mattick wrote at the close of the Second World War: "Today every programme and designation has lost its meaning; socialists speak in capitalistic terms, capitalists in socialistic terms and everybody believes anything and nothing. This situation is merely the climax of a long development which has been initiated by the labour movement itself. . . . Only by standing outside the labour movement has it been possible to work towards decisive social changes."[2]

The first condition for a minimum revolutionary action is indeed to "stand outside" and break with all forms of Marxism, whether they come from CPs or left-wing intellectuals. Marxism is part of capitalist society in its theory as well as its practice.[3]

Nowadays, when the long counter-revolution which followed the post-1917 revolutionary movement is finally coming to a close, a new movement is rising.[4] At the same time, capital is trying to defang it, and is preparing to destroy it violently if it cannot be deflected. The re-emergence of revolution is accompanied by many forms of superficial criticism which do not go to the heart of the matter, and help capital adapt itself. Obviously radicalisation results from diverse experiences. But pseudo-revolutionary groups deliberately gather people on partial demands in order to prevent them to go any further. They claim to go back to revolutionary principles, but are ignorant of them. At best, their view of communism mixes a partial social re-shuffling with democratic worker control or management, plus automation. In other words, no more than what capital itself talks about. They "critically" support the official CPs, socialist parties, the USSR, China, Cuba, etc. These groups are counter-revolutionary. The argument that they organise workers is irrelevant: CPs do the same, which does not prevent them from repressing workers when they think it necessary. Trotskyism, Maoism, even anarchism in some bureaucratic and degenerated forms, are counter-revolutionary.

Past experience shows why demarcation lines are necessary. In 1939, the capitalist system could only recover through a full-scale worldwide war. Russia had been forced to develop capitalism after the defeat of revolution in Europe, and was ready to ally with one side or the other according to its State interests. Germany, Italy, and Japan were fascist. In the Western democracies, socialist and "communist" parties managed to rally the masses and persuaded them that unlike 1914–18, the new world war was to free mankind from the horrors of dictatorship. Trotskyism also supported this view and most Trotskyists took the side of the allied powers against Germany and Japan. Yet the triumph of democracy in 1945 has proved destructive. People no longer die in concentration camps—except where there are concentration camps, as in Russia, China, etc. But millions starve. The extreme left

(Trotsky and many others) had helped capitalism rejuvenate itself.

Marx had to fight against Proudhon. Lenin, Pannekoek, Bordiga had to fight against Kautsky. Pannekoek and Bordiga had to fight against Lenin, and later against Trotsky.[5]

The present communist movement needs to assimilate its past, to fully grasp what really happened in 1917–21 and how today differs from yesterday. Communist revolution will not promote a further development of production: capital has already accomplished this in a large number of countries. The transitional phase will consist of the immediate communisation of society, which includes armed insurrection: the State's military might cannot be underestimated. Besides, the working class has become such a potential social force that it is vital for capitalism to control it: this is the job of the unions and workers' parties, so one must prepare to confront them.

This is only possible through the implementation of the communist programme: abolition of the market economy; creation of new social relations where labour does not rule the whole of life, but is integrated into it; destruction of economics as such, of politics as such, of art as such, etc.

Speaking of theory, one can and must use Marx's works (which includes translating and publishing them when they are not available). Our motto is: Do not read the Marxists, read Marx![6] It is also useful to study those who resisted counter-revolution: people like Pannekoek, Bordiga, etc., who despite misconceptions are relevant to our problems. Other groups, like the Situationist International, are also important, though they lack an understanding of capital.[7] Also it is important for revolutionaries everywhere to study the revolutionary past of their country.

Such activity implies a break with politics. Revolutionaries do not only have different ideas (or even actions) from pseudo-revolutionaries. What they *are* is different, and the way they act is. They do not try to enrol people in order to represent them and be a power in their name. Revolutionaries are not leaders, educators, memory keepers or information providers. We neither lead nor serve the proles.

Communists are not isolated from the proletariat. Their action is never an attempt to organise others, only to express their own subversive response to the world. Ultimately, revolutionary initiatives will interconnect. But our task is not primarily one of organisation: it is to convey (in a text or an action) an antagonistic relation to the world. However big or small it may be, such an act is an attack against the old world.

■ FOREWORD TO THE 1974 BLACK & RED EDITION

Small changes have been made and new notes added.

In spite of its shortcomings, the Situationist International has shown—among other things—that it is important not just to understand the historical movement and act accordingly, but also *to be* something different from the attitudes and values of the society the revolutionary wants to destroy. The *militant* attitude is anti-revolutionary: it splits the individual into two, separating his needs, his real individual and social self, the reasons why he cannot stand the present world, from his action, his attempt to change this world. The militant refuses to admit that he rebels against this society because he needs to change his own life as well as society in general. He represses the impulse which made him turn against the present world. He engages in anti-capitalist activity as if it were external to him: the sacrificial character of this attitude is plain to see. The militant as an individual, and political groups as organisations, suffer from a displaced personality.[1]

Whatever the situation may have been fifty or a hundred years ago, the present revolutionary movement does not aim to bring about the conditions of communism: these have been fully created by capitalism. Our objective is no longer to further promote the development of productive forces or to maintain and support this development with coercive action by the proletariat over the petite bourgeoisie: it is the immediate communisation of society. Capital has managed to invade and dominate our lives to such an extent that—at least in so-called developed countries—we are now revolutionary because we can no longer stand our relationship to our work, our friend, our environment, namely to everything from our next-door neighbour to our cat or radio programme. We want to change the world because it becomes increasingly difficult to realise and assert oneself in it. Our most vital need: others, seems so close and so far at the same time. A human community is at hand: its basis is present, a lot more so than a century ago. Passivity prevents its emergence. Mercantile ties are both fragile and strong.

Capitalism reacts by diverting social impulses from revolution to politics: revolutionary activity which strives to realise people's needs is deviated towards a mere quest for power. For instance, people want to control their own lives, which are now regulated by the logic of commodity production and value. Political groups come and explain that the alternative is real democracy, or workers' government, or even anarchy-inspired institutions: in other words, they wish to alter the decision-making apparatus, not the social relations which determine it. They always reduce social aspirations to a problem of control or command, which ought to be given to a proletarian party, or to the masses, or shared by everyone, and they express every real problem in terms of power.

Yet this is only part of the question. Communising society is more than a sum of piecemeal actions. Though capital will be destroyed by general subversion through which people appropriate their relationship to the world, nothing decisive will be achieved so long as the State (i.e. all States) retains some of its power. The State has to be destroyed by acting on its central bodies in addition to the action which destroys its power everywhere. Both are necessary. The use of force is a relevant question: insurrection won't be peaceful and non-violent.

Capital would be only too happy to see us change our lives locally while its active process continues on a general scale. This is not a moot point: many people are desperate to modify their personal life *now*, even it boils down to a remodelled lifestyle. Capitalism can tolerate a lot (decomposition of the traditional family and hierarchy, even of mercantile relations on a limited scale) as long as these changes do not prevent it from realising its cycle, from accumulating value. The coming revolution will paralyse it by developing direct communist relations *and* by systematic action against State bodies and private bourgeois militia.[2]

As for the present, what we can do is reject all forms of militantism and politics, all groups standing as mediations between the proletariat and communism, and which believe and make people believe in political solutions.

Such groups are of course different from one country to another. In France and Italy, the traditional Communist Parties are very powerful, and the unions they control differ from North American, British, or northern European unions.[3] Therefore the text on "The Class Struggle and Its Most Characteristic Aspects" might seem irrelevant to the American, German, or English contexts. But the essential process is the same. When we speak of the end of reformism we refer to a general trend, and do not mean that reformist struggles are becoming rare. On the contrary, many people, inside and outside the working class, are fighting for reforms, but these struggles are manifestations of something deeper. Though few strikes are similar to the one at Lordstown in the United States (1972), such an event was symptomatic of a social tendency.[4]

The relative backwardness of France and Italy in relation to the United States or Britain has created a number of mediators which play a more open role than in other countries. In the still fairly traditional and formal French or Italian politics, the left and the far left are hardened bodies which pretend to oppose the State. They still retain some ability to organise people. In other countries, many extremist groups have disappeared, the American and German SDS for example.[5]

The difficulty lies in the need to go beyond traditional "Marxism" while not rejecting relevant concepts. It is not enough to understand that Marcuse, Mandel, Sweezy, and Magdoff have hardly anything in common with communism.[6] Breaking new ground means drawing a line between what to rubbish and where to begin a thorough re-think.

The nub of the debate is how we envisage communism. For example, underdeveloped countries—to use a capitalist vocabulary—will not have to go through an industrialisation phase similar to what advanced countries experienced in the past. In many parts of Asia, Africa, and Latin America, capital has not yet completely subjugated labour to its domination. Old forms of social life still exist (for how long?). Communism will give them a new birth—with the help of "Western" technology, applied totally differently from the way it was used in the West. We cannot be content with a mere demonstration of the capitalist nature of China and North Vietnam: we must also just as clearly assess the role Asia could play in a future revolution. The Ceylon uprising of 1971 was indeed a modern movement.[7] Utopia is back. We can already hear news from everywhere.

■ FOREWORLD:
OUT OF THE FUTURE (1997)

This was the preface to the Antagonism Press edition in London (1997).
Some changes and additions have been made to the text and notes.

1) The Untraceable

One of the best films about class conflict includes a ten-minute sharp and biting shot, taken on June 10, 1968, outside the gates of the Wonder factory—a battery-maker—on the outskirts of Paris.[1] Most of the workers were unskilled, low-paid, looked-down-upon women, often handling dirty chemicals. They'd been on strike since May 13th and were just about to go back in. What concessions they'd snatched from the boss were a lot in terms of better work conditions, and little compared to the energy put into the struggle. In the middle of the arguing group is a woman in her twenties—half shouting, half crying—who won't be talked into returning: "No, I'm not going back. I'll never set foot there again! Go and see for yourself what a shit-hole it is . . . what filth we work in . . ."

In 1996, a documentary interviewed people involved in that strike: men and women workers, foremen, a Trotskyist typist, shop stewards, union activists, the local Communist Party leader who tried to convince the young woman to resume work. She, however, is untraceable. Few remember her well. She left the factory soon after the events and nobody knows what became of her, or even her full name, only the first one: Jocelyne.

We're left with one decisive question unanswered, the question posed by Jocelyne's reaction: in "normal" peaceful life, habits and guidelines weigh upon us, and it is practically inevitable to submit. But when millions of strikers build up collective strength, render the State helpless and media words worthless, bring a whole country to the verge of overall change, and realise they're given pay rises which will soon be eaten up by inflation, why is it that they step back into what they know amounts to dire or soft misery for the next twenty years?

Many a radical school of thought will come up with its ready-made answer and solution. Some will reply that Jocelyne and her workmates had been betrayed by the wrong sort of leaders, or brainwashed by the media, or manipulated by the unions, some will assert workers suffered from an absence of organisation, others that they lacked spontaneity and autonomy, while wise guys will explain May '68 was bound to fail because capitalist evolution had not yet created the prerequisites of the conditions of true communist revolution, which fortunately are now coming to full maturation . . . .

This is no maths exercise where you have to find the right clue. In the words of a Persian poet, "this deep riddle will ne'er be solved by science and research."[2] The following essays merely ask this first and foremost question:

How does class struggle (under capitalism, history's prime mover) connect with human emancipation which goes beyond class? Class struggle concerns us in so far as it can produce its own end: communism. As we know, that struggle can also feed on itself, forcing the capital-labour relation to change, to get both softer and stronger, and this is what class struggle does most of the time.

The crux of communist theory is to know if, how, and when the proletarians wage a class struggle that is able to produce more than itself.

Communist revolution is not just an intensified extension of the labour v. capital confrontation: it *intensifies* this confrontation and *breaks away* from it.

One of the texts, "The Class Struggle and Its Most Characteristic Aspects in Recent Years," was first conceived not long after the Wonder plant, like many others, returned to work. "Leninism and the Ultra-Left" goes back to 1969. "Capitalism and Communism" came out in 1972 at the request of a number of workers who circulated the first draft, at the Paris Renault plant among others.

2) Wall Street v. Berlin Wall

These three essays aimed at reasserting communism against an ideology named "Marxism"—official, leftist, or academic.

Why call ourselves communist?

The more a lexical item means, the more likely it is to be put into hard labour by the ruling order.[3]

Like "freedom," "autonomy," "humanity," and a host of other words, *communism* has been twisted, turned upside down, and is currently a synonym of life under a benevolent/dictatorial totalitarian State. Only a free, autonomous, human, communist awakening will make these words meaningful again.

Although common wisdom proclaims that radical thought is obsolete, the last twenty-five years offer ample proof of its relevance.

What obsolescence?!

Class and *class struggle?* No need to read two thousand pages by Marx to realise that those dispossessed of the means of production have fought (and so far been defeated by) those who control them. In the early nineteenth century, a utopian socialist reformer like Saint-Simon as well as academics were among the first to theorise *class*: bourgeois historians analysed the French revolution as the conflict between aristocracy and bourgeoisie. Two hundred years later, the strength of the ruling class is to make us forget it exists.

Value defined by the average social time necessary to manufacture goods? It's plain our civilisation has an obsession with shortening time. Computerisation, electronic highways and cell phones on every street corner speed up circulation. Work, shopping, and leisure alike treat every act of life as though it had to be turned into an ever-faster flow. Paul Virilio describes how economy does not produce just objects but speed, and indeed objects only as far as they produce speed. Though his stance is completely different from Marx's, Virilio points at a world that prides itself on reducing the time needed to achieve everything, i.e. a world run by minimal time—by value.[4]

Profit making as the driving force of this world? Anyone who has lost his job in a firm he gave twenty years of his life to, can see that a company is accumulated value constantly looking for its own accretion and crushing whatever hinders it.

The decreasing numbers of Western factory workers, the coming down of the Berlin Wall, and the withering away of far-left groups mean the final downfall of communism only to those who portrayed blue collar workers as the salt of the earth, equated socialism with planned economy, and enjoyed marching in the street under the North Vietnam flag.

The collapse of so-called socialist countries proved how economy rules. East and West have both gone through accumulation crises. Trying to regain profitability required a new system of production in Cleveland, a new political regime in Moscow. State capitalism did not fail because people got fed up with totalitarianism, but when it was no longer able to support itself and give substance to its oppression.

Centralised economic planning was just about all right for developing capital goods industries; and bureaucratic power rested on a compromise with the peasants on the one hand (after the horrors of forced collectivisation, the kolkhoznik was left free to attend to his allotment), and the workers on the other (job for life plus minimal social security, in exchange for political submission). This unspoken bargain may have been OK for Russia in 1930, but not in 1980, let alone for East Germany or Czechoslovakia in 1980. Capitalism needs some degree of competition between conflicting poles of accumulated value confronting each other, and a certain dose of political competition as well. Eventually State-led capitalism exhausted its propulsive force and even bureaucrats no longer believed their own lies.

The breaking up of the USSR is not the definitive refutation of Marx, but the verification of *Das Kapital*. The Politburo could fiddle its own internal market but not evade world trade pressures. The same market forces that were laying off thousands in Liverpool were busy smashing the bureaucratic dykes that blocked the streams of money and commodities in Leningrad. The spectre still haunts us, the *Wall Street Journal* wrote in 1991, in reference to the 1848 *Manifesto*: "Marx's analysis can be applied to the amazing disintegration of communist regimes built on the foundations of his thought but unfaithful to his prescriptions."

3) 1968 and All That

There had been workers' uprisings before, openly confronting both the State and the institutionalised labour movement, and many far more violent, after 1917 for example. But around 1970, the upheaval had something more global and deeper about it. Contrary to 1871, 1917–21 or 1936–37, capital had penetrated the whole of life in industrialised countries, turned more and more everyday acts and relationships into commodities, and unified society under its dominion. Politics as the confrontation of utterly opposed political programmes was on the way out. In '68, French unions and labour parties were able to stifle a four or five-million three-week strike, but could no longer put forward a platform alternative to that of "bourgeois" parties. Those who had taken part in the general strike did not expect much more from a possible left government than a more generous welfare. Mixed economy was the order of the day, with an emphasis on State intervention when the left was in power, on market forces when votes swung to the right.

In the 1960s less than now, but a lot more than before the 1939–45 war, commodity relationships mediated the simplest human needs. The American dream is yours if you're rich enough to buy it: even so, the most desirable car is never the one you've just bought, rather the next one on the TV commercial. Goods are always at their best on posters. Just when a Russian-style workers' paradise was no longer valid, the consumer heaven appeared out of reach. So no future could be found through the factory, neither the nightmare the other side of the Iron Curtain, nor the dreamland this side of the screen. As a result, the workplace declined as a place where to start building a better world. Although the Situationist *Society of the Spectacle* had few readers at the time, its publication in 1967 was a forerunner of critiques to come. True, that period also meant unionisation for many downtrodden poorly paid workers who finally got into the twentieth century, and only a minority of the working class voiced a refusal of society, rebels with a cause on the fringe of the labour force, the young especially. But the worldwide strike and riot wave remains incomprehensible without its underlying characteristic: mass disaffection for factory and office life. "Who wants to work?" *Newsweek* asked in the mid-1970s.

Still, nearly all sit-downs occupied the workplace and went no further. There were many transgressing gestures: takeover of gas and transport services by Polish strikers in 1971, Italian self-reduction, squatting, "giveaway" "social" strikes by bus drivers, hospital staff, and supermarket cashiers providing transport, health care, and food free of charge, electricity workers cutting off supplies to bureaucrats or firms, and a thousand other instances. Yet hardly any turned into a beginning of communisation. The disruption of work and the trespassing of commodity did not merge into an attack on work-as-commodity, i.e. wage labour as such. From prison to child education, everything came under fire, yet the assault remained mainly negative.

The lack of creative attempts to transform society gave the impetus back to capitalism.

Historical upheavals have no date of birth or death, but surely Fiat was more than a symbol—a landmark. For years the Turin firm had been plagued by permanent stoppages of assembly lines, mass absenteeism and meetings on the premises. However, organised disorder did not transcend negation into something positive. Thus the management was able to break a (fairly large) minority, with the passive help of a weary majority fearing for their jobs. Radicals had disrupted a social logic, not shifted into a new one. Violent (even armed) actions gradually disconnected from the shop floor. In 1980, the company laid off 23,000 out of 140,000: the factory went on strike for thirty-five days, until a mix of 40,000 Fiat workers, clerks, and middle managers took to the streets against the strike. The unions signed a compromise whereby the 23,000 got State compensation money, and later many more thousands were sacked through rationalisation. On such turning points was the social surge of the 1960s–70s reversed.

Logically, worker class defeat was translated into political terms, on all sides of the political spectrum. On the right, Thatcher and Reagan epitomised the liberal swing. On the left, the French Socialist Party came to power in 1981, only to turn to austerity after two years. British Labour embraced market economics. The Italy CP used to get as much as 30 percent of overall vote in the 1970s: it gradually gave up any extremist appearances, became the Party of the Democratic Left, dropped the hammer and sickle, evolved into the Democrats of the left and later a mere Democratic Party.

4) Working Man's Blues

Since then, the defeats of the European, North American, and Japanese working class have been due to its defensive position against a constantly mobile opponent. However deeply entrenched in mines or workshops, workers' militancy could not resist restructuring. Labour is strong as long as it's necessary to capital. Otherwise, it can delay redundancy, sometimes for years with support from the rest of the working community, but it can't stay on for ever as an unprofitable labour force. In the 1970s and '80s workers had number and organisation, later they lost because the economy deprived them of their function, which is their social weapon. As proved by the

English miners' strike in 1984–85, nothing will force capital to hire labour that is not useful to it, and ten years later there were more university lecturers than miners in England.[5]

For years, assembly line workers had rejected being treated like human robots, while a minority turned away from work and the consumer society. Capital replied by installing mechanical robots, suppressing millions of jobs and revamping, intensifying, densifying what was left of unskilled labour. At the same time, a widespread desire for freedom was converted into freedom to buy. In 1960, who imagined that one day a twelve-year-old could get cash out of a dispenser with her own plastic card? Her money—her freedom . . . The famous slogans of '68: *Never work!* and *Ask for the impossible!* were mocked when people were forced out of secure jobs and offered ever more plentiful and frustrating goods to buy . . . often on credit.

Many compare today's situation to the 1920s and '30s— fascist threat included.[6] However, unlike the insurrections and armed counter-revolution that took place between 1917 and 1937, the present proletarian setback has been a protracted and gradual absorption of vast sections of the working class into joblessness and casualisation. "If there was hope, it must lie in the proles," Winston said in *1984*. It's as though a lot of the proles of the real 1984 year had been fighting for two decades, nearly taken the world into their hands but refused either to accept or change it until the impetus ran out of steam. In the 1920s, their grandfathers had locked themselves behind factory gates, sometimes with guns (Italy, 1920), fought and died, and class conflict ended up with bosses' victory.[7] This time only a handful got their guns (and even less with mass unemployment: one does not shoot at a closing plant). So, more a failure than a defeat, actually. Like a player stepping aside from a fixed game: he can't or won't smash the place, and lets the fixers win.

That game was lost, there's no use denying it. Capitalism triumphs, more fluid and immaterial than twenty-five years ago, universalising everything in an abstract, passive, screen-wise, negative way. A '60s commercial, reproduced in *Situationist International* no. 7, pictured factory workers commenting a newspaper page with an advertisement for a washing machine, and wondering: "Who makes this model?" Forcibly part-time or flexible, the year 2000 car worker will watch *Crash* on TV while his kid plays a video game that uses chips which could one day "downsize" his father or himself. Never before has humankind been so unified and divided. Billions watch the same pictures and live ever more separate lives. Goods are at the same time mass produced and unavailable. In 1930, millions were out of work because of a huge economic breakdown. Now millions are on the dole, the economy cannot make profits out of them as it did in the post-1945 recovery, the profitability crisis of the 1970s is not over, and labour productivity has risen so much that capital needs less labour to valorise itself.

5) High Hopes . . .

The workers' movement that existed in 1900, or still in 1936, was neither crushed by fascist repression nor bought off by transistors or fridges: it destroyed itself as a force of change because it aimed at preserving the proletarian condition, not superseding it. At best it got a better life for the toiling masses: that seemed to tame the system . . . before the system produced its worst in the form of two world wars.

The worker movement as we knew it is now as dead as British Old Labour, and the popularity of films about workers' culture is a sure sign of its passing from reality into memories and museums. Stalinists turn social-democrat and social democracy goes centre-left. Everybody shifts to the right and soon Trotskyists will name themselves radical democrats.[8] As for us, we won't feel nostalgic about a time when crowds paraded the streets singing "The Internationale" when they were in fact supporting groups trying to be the extreme-left of the left.

The purpose of the old labour movement was to take over the same world and manage it in a new way: forcing the *leisure class* to work, turning unproductive into productive work, developing industry, introducing workers' democracy (in theory, of course). Only a tiny minority, "anarchist" as well as "Marxist," held that a different society meant the destruction of State, commodity, and wage labour, although it rarely defined this as a process, rather as a programme to put into practice *after* the seizure of power, often after a fairly long transition period. These revolutionaries failed to grasp communism as a social movement whose action would undermine the foundations of class and State power, and misunderstood the subversive potential of fraternal, open, communistic relationships that kept re-emerging in every deep insurrection (Russia 1917–19, Catalonia 1936–37 . . .).

There is no need to create the capitalist preconditions of communism any more. Capitalism is everywhere, yet much less visible than one hundred or fifty years ago when class distinctions ostensibly showed up. The manual worker identified the factory owner at one glance, knew or thought he knew his enemy, and felt he'd be better off the day he and his mates got rid of the boss. Today classes still exist, but manifested through infinite degrees in consumption, and no-one expects a better world from public ownership of industry. The "enemy" is an impalpable social relationship, abstract yet real, all-pervading yet no monster beyond our reach: because the proletarians are the ones that produce and reproduce the world, they can disrupt and revolutionise it. The aim of a future revolution will be immediate communisation, not fully completed before a generation or more, but to be started from the beginning. Capital has invaded life, and determines how we eat, sleep, love, visit, or bury friends, to such an extent that our objective can only be the social fabric, invisible, all-encompassing. Although capital is quite good at hiring personnel to defend it, social inertia is a greater conservative force than media or police.

The 1991 Los Angeles riots went further than those of Watts in 1965. The succession of estate riots shows a significant fraction of youth cannot be integrated. Here and there, in spite of mass unemployment, workers won't be black-mailed into accepting lower wages as barter against job crea-tion. South Korean factory workers have proved the "World Company" spreads shop-floor restlessness at the same time as it accumulates windfall profits, and "backward" Albania gave birth to a modern rising in 1997.[9] When a sizeable minor-ity fed up with virtual reality starts making possibilities real, revolution will rise again, terrible and anonymous.

This is dedicated to Jocelyne, the unknown worker.

CHAPTER 1

■ CAPITALISM AND COMMUNISM

The first 1972 version of this essay underwent various changes in 1997. It has been considerably modified again for this new edition.

Communism is not a programme one puts into practice or makes others put into practice, but a social movement. Apart from perhaps a clearer understanding, those who develop and defend theoretical communism are moved by the same practical personal need for communism as those who are not especially concerned by theory. They have no privilege whatsoever: they do not carry the knowledge that will set the revolution in motion. On the other hand, they have no fear of taking initiatives. Like every other revolution, the communist revolution is the product of real living conditions and desires. The points made in this text are born out of social contradictions and practical struggles which help us discern the possibilities of a new society amidst and against the monstrosity and fascination of the old.

Communism is not an ideal to be realised: it already exists, not as alternative lifestyles, autonomous zones or counter-communities that would grow within this society and ultimately change it into another one, but as an effort, a task to prepare for. It is the movement which tries to abolish the conditions of life determined by wage-labour, and it will abolish them only by revolution.

We will not refute the CPs, the various brands of social-ists, the far left, etc., whose programmes call for a modernisa-tion and democratisation of all existing features of the present world. The point is not that these programmes do not go far enough, but that they stay within the boundaries of the present society: they are capitalist programmes.

1) Wage-Labour as a Social Relation

If one looks at modern society, it is obvious that in order to live, the great majority of people are forced to sell their labour power. All the physical and intellectual capacities existing in human beings, in their personalities, which must be set in motion to produce useful things, can only be used if they are sold in exchange for wages. Labour power is usually perceived as a commodity bought and sold nearly like all others. The existence of exchange and wage-labour seems normal, inevi-table. Yet the introduction of wage-labour involved conflict, resistance, and bloodshed. The separation of the worker from the means of production, now an accepted fact of life, took a long time and was accomplished by force.

In England, in the Netherlands, in France, from the six-teenth century on, economic and political violence expro-priated craftsmen and peasants, repressed indigence and vagrancy, imposed wage-labour on the poor. Between 1930 and 1950, Russia decreed a labour code which included capital punishment in order to organise the transition of millions of peasants to industrial wage-labour in less than a few decades. Seemingly normal facts: that an individual has nothing but his labour power, that he must sell it to a business unit to be able to live, that everything is a commodity, that social relations revolve around market exchange ... such facts now taken for granted result from a long, brutal process.

By means of its school system and its ideological and political life, contemporary society hides the past and present violence on which this situation rests. It conceals both its origin and the mechanism which enables it to function. Everything appears as a free contract in which the individual, as a seller of labour power, encounters the factory, the shop or the office. The existence of the commodity seems to be an obvious and natural phenomenon, and the periodic major and minor disasters it causes are often regarded as quasi-natural calamities. Goods are destroyed to maintain their prices, existing capacities are left to rot, while elementary needs remain unfulfilled. Yet the main thing that the system hides is not the existence of exploitation or class (that is not too hard to see), nor its horrors (modern society is quite good at turning them into media show). It is not even that the wage labour/capital relationship causes unrest and rebellion (that also is fairly plain to see). The main thing it conceals is that insubordination and revolt could be large and deep enough to do away with this relationship and make another world possible.

What characterises human society is the fact that it produces and reproduces the material conditions of its existence. Other forms of life—bees, for example—make their own material conditions, but, at least as far as we can understand them, their evolution remains at a timeless standstill. Human activity is a continually changing appropriation and assimilation of man's environment. In other words, humankind has a history. The relation of humans to "nature" is also a relation among humans and depends on their relations of production, just as the ideas they produce, the way they conceive the world, depend on their production relations.

Production relations into which people enter are independent of their will: each generation confronts technical and social conditions left by previous generations. But it can alter them. What we call "history" is made by people. This is not to say that the windmill created the feudal lord, the steam engine the bourgeois industrialist and that, in due time, with the same implacable logic, automation and electronics will free the toiling masses. If this were true, there would be no revolutions. The new society bred by the old can only emerge through a violent decisive break through the entire social, political, and ideological structure.

What must be exposed, behind the material objects, the machines, the factories, the labourers who work there every day, the things they produce, is the social relation that regulates them, as well as its necessary and possible evolution.

2) "Value" as a Destroyer . . . and Promoter of Community

What is known as "the primitive community" matters to us because it shows that the rule of money is a historical—not natural—reality, far less widespread and fairly more recent than we are usually taught. But there is no point in eulogising it. Superficial critics of contemporary capitalism would like to get rid of its bad side (cars, banks, cops . . .) while developing the good side (cycling lanes, schools, hospitals . . .). Similarly, though many primitivists would certainly appreciate the harmony with nature enjoyed by the Native Americans portrayed in *Dances with Wolves*, few would tolerate living under the domination of patriarchy and myth. While the North American *potlatch* happened in a non-market environment, it went along with hierarchy and power.

Anyway, there is no going back: we will not re-enact the past.

As far as anthropology is to be trusted, it seems that human beings first lived in relatively autonomous and scattered groups, in families (in the broadest sense: the family grouping all those of the same blood), in clans or tribes. Production consisted essentially of hunting, fishing, and gathering. There was no individual production, as the individual did not exist, nor freedom as we are used to it. Activities were decided (actually imposed on the group by the group) and achieved in common, and their results shared in common. Not everyone got a "fair" share, but "production" and "consumption" took place without the mediation of comparing separately produced goods.

Many a "primitive" community had the "technical" means to accumulate surpluses and simply did not bother. As M. Sahlins pointed out, the age of scarcity often meant abundance, with lots of idle time—though our "time" would have

34

had little relevance to these people.[1] As the West explored and conquered the world, travellers and anthropologists observed that searching for and storing food took a rather small portion of a "primitive's" day. After calculating that in just one hour, in the eighteenth century, an English farmer produced 2,600 calories and some Indonesians 4,500, Gregory Clark draws a parallel with hunter-gatherers who only "worked" a few hours a day: "Thus the average person in the world of 1800 was no better off than the person of 100,000 BC."[2] Quite a striking comparison, but is it relevant to use the same notion, *work*, for a Papuan hunter-gatherer and a Yorkshire rural day-labourer? Clark has the mindset of an economist. The main point is that primitive "productive" activity was part of a global relationship with the group and its environment.

Eventually, not all but most of humankind moved from hunting-gathering into agriculture and ended up developing surpluses, which communities started swapping.

This circulation was achieved by taking into account what is common to all goods. The products of human activity have this one thing in common: every one of them results from a certain amount of exertion of physical and mental effort. Labour has an abstract character: it does not only produce a useful thing, it also consumes energy, both individual and social. The *value* of a product, independently of its use, is the quantity of abstract labour it contains, i.e. the quantity of social energy necessary to reproduce it. Since this quantity can only be measured in terms of the time spent, the value of a product is the time socially necessary to produce it, namely the average for a given society at a given moment in its history.

With the growth of its activities and needs, the community came to produce not only goods, but also commodities, goods produced to be exchanged, and for their exchange value. Commerce first appeared between communities, then penetrated inside communities, giving rise to specialised activities, trades, socially divided labour. The very nature of labour changed. Productive activity was no longer integrated into the totality of social activity: it became a specialised field, separated from the rest of the individual's life. What somebody makes for himself is set apart from what he makes for the purpose of exchange. The second part of his activity means sacrifice, time-counting, working hours as opposed to free time, and constraint: society becomes not just diversified into different trades, it is divided between workers and *non*-workers. Work is *class*.

Exchange relations help the community to develop and to satisfy its growing needs, but they ultimately destroy what made the community immediately communal. People now treat each other, and themselves, mainly as suppliers of goods. The utility of the product I make for exchange no longer interests me: I am only interested in the utility of the product I will get in exchange. But for the person who sells it to me, this second utility does not matter: his sole concern lies in the usefulness of what I produced. What is use value for the one is only exchange value for the other, and vice versa.

Community started to erode when its members became interested in each other only to the extent that they benefited from each other. Not that altruism was the driving force of the primitive community, or should be the driving force of communism. But in one case the movement of interests drives persons together and makes them act in common, whereas in the other it individualises them and compels them to be indifferent or antagonistic to one another. Even when we do not treat each other as enemies, most daily encounters are ruled by the urge to save time and "get things done." With the birth of value exchange in the community, labour is no longer the realisation of needs by a collective, but the means to obtain from others the satisfaction of one's needs.

While it developed exchange, the community tried to restrain it. It attempted to control or destroy surpluses or to establish strict rules to control the circulation of goods. Some Ancient Greeks opposed *economics*, i.e. exchanging goods between producers at a "fair price" (what could now be called "the real economy"), to *chrematistics*, accumulating wealth for its own sake. For a long while, only a fraction of exchange was based on value, viz. on a reasonably sound calculation of equivalent average labour time. Nevertheless, value triumphed in the end. Wherever it did not, society withdrew into itself until it was eventually crushed by the invasion of merchant conquerors.

As long as goods are not produced separately, as long as there is no division of labour, one does not and cannot compare the respective values of two items, since they are produced and distributed in common. The moment of exchange, during which the labour times of two products are measured and the products exchanged accordingly, does not exist yet. The abstract character of labour appears only when within human groups, some members trade their products with each other and also with other groups. With these two prerequisites, value, i.e. average labour time, becomes the instrument of measure.

Value is a linkage, because the average socially necessary labour time is the one element all different tasks have in common: they all have the property of consuming a certain quantity of human labour power, regardless of the particular way in which this power is used. Corresponding to the abstract character of labour, value represents its abstraction, its general and social character, apart from all differences in nature between the objects labour produces.

Value was not born because it is a convenient instrument of measure. It appeared as an indispensable mediation of human activities because these activities were separated and had to be linked by some means of comparison. Labour became *work*, viz. a physical or mental effort meant to be as productive as possible, not in the interest of the worker, but for the benefit of the one who was putting him to work and profiting from it. It is not technique we are talking about, but social division: class. Work is inseparable from the fact that a group has no other way of subsistence than working for a group who controls the means of production.

A new sort of community was born: with the autonomi-sation of value, *via wage-labour*, "money appears in fact as the thing-like existing community" (Marx).[3]

3) Commodity

Up to our time included (so far), with the advance of the effi-ciency of human organisation and its capacity to associate the components of the labour process, first of all labour power, history has coincided with the difference (and the opposition) between those who work and those who organise work and profit from it. The first towns and great irrigation projects were born out of an increased productive efficiency. Commerce appeared as a special activity: some people do not make a living by producing, but by mediating between the various activities of the separate units of production. An increasing proportion of items, artefacts, places, ideas, emotions, sou-venirs become commodities. To be used, to put into practice their ability to fulfil a need, they must be bought, they must fulfil their exchange value. Otherwise, although they exist materially, they do not exist socially, and no-one has a right to use them, because commodity is not just a thing, but first and foremost a social relation ruled by the logic of exchange. Use value is the support of value. Production becomes a sphere distinct from consumption, and work a sphere distinct from non-work. Private property is the legal framework of the sepa-ration between activities, between men, between units of pro-duction. The slave is a commodity for his owner, who buys a man to work for him, whereas the wage-labourer is his *own* private proprietor, legally free to choose who to work for, at least in principle and in democratic capitalism.

Money made value "visible" and transferable (though coinage was unknown until the seventh century BC). The abstraction, value, is materialised in money, becomes a commodity, and tends to become independent, to detach itself from what it comes from and represents: use values, real goods. Compared to simple exchange (x quantity of product A against y quantity of product B), money permits a universalisation, where anything can be obtained for a quantity of abstract labour time crystallised in money. Money is labour time abstracted from labour and solidified in a durable, measurable, transportable form. Money is the visible, tangible manifestation of the common element in all commodities— not two or several commodities, but all possible commodities. Money allows its owner to command the work of others, any time any place in the world. With money it is possible to escape from the constraints of time and space.

A tendency towards a universal economy occurred around some great centres from Ancient times to the Middle Ages, but it failed to reach its aim. The propensity of empires to overstretch, and their subsequent break-up or destruction, illustrate this succession of failures.[4] Rome was not the only huge geopolitical entity to rise and fall. Exchange relations periodically came to an end between the various parts of the *civilised* (i.e. statist and mercantile) world, after the demise of one or several empires. Such interruptions might last for centuries, during which the economy seemed to go backwards, towards a subsistence economy, until gold and sword combined to generate another aspiring all-encompassing power. Commerce alone, simple commodity production could not provide the stability, the durability required by the socialisation and unification of the world. Only capitalism created, from the sixteenth century on, but mainly in the nineteenth and twentieth centuries, the necessary basis for a durable world-unified economy, when the Industrial Revolution turned *labour* itself into the Number One commodity.

4) Capital

Capital is a production relation which establishes a completely new and dramatically efficient bond between living labour and past labour (accumulated by previous generations). In several Western European countries after the Middle Ages, merchants had accumulated large sums of money, perfected systems of banking and credit, and found possible to use these sums by hiring labour to work on machines. Masses of former peasants or craftsmen dispossessed (by debt or brute force) of their instruments of production were forced to work as wage-labourers on accumulated, stored-up labour in the form of machines, particularly in the textile industry. Past labour was set in motion by the living labour of those who had not been able to realise such an accumulation of raw materials and means of production.

There is *no valorisation without work*. Labour power is quite a special commodity: its consumption furnishes work, hence new value, whereas means of production yield no more than their own value. Therefore the use of labour power furnishes a supplementary value. The origin of bourgeois wealth is to be found in this surplus value, in the difference between the value created by the wage-labourer in his work, and the value necessary for the reproduction of his labour-power. Wages only cover the expenses of that reproduction (the means of subsistence of the worker and his family).

Past labour is valorised by living labour. To invest, to accumulate—these are the mottos of capital, and the priority given to heavy industry in "socialist" countries is a sure sign of capitalism. But the system only multiplies steel mills, mines, airports, docks, etc., if and when they help accumulate value. Capital is first of all a sum of value, of abstract labour crystallised in the form of money, finance capital, shares, bonds, etc., in search for its own expansion, preferably in *liquid* form which makes capital as universally transferable as can be. An x sum of value must give $x + profit$ at the end of the cycle.

The appropriation of surplus-value by the bourgeois is an integral part of the system, which is logically run by the class who benefits from it. But this inevitable fact is not the heart of the matter. Supposing the capitalist and the wage-labourer were fused into one, if labour truly managed capital, re-oriented production in the interest of everyone, if wages were equal and fair, etc., *and value logic continued to operate*, it would not go beyond capitalism: it would be a (short-lived) worker-led capitalism.

The point is not that a handful of people take a dispro-
portionately large share of surplus-value. If these parasitic
profiteers were pushed aside, while the rest of the system
remained, part of the surplus-value would be given to the
workers and the rest invested in collective and social equipment, welfare, etc.: this is the age-old programme of the left,
including the official CPs. Unfortunately, the logic of the value
system involves developing production for maximal valorisation. In a society based on value, value dominates society, not
the other way round. The change brought about by capital
is to have conquered production, and thus to have socialised
the world since the nineteenth century, spreading industrial
plants, warehouses, ports, telecommunication networks, etc.,
all over the world, which results in goods being available in
shops. But in the capitalist cycle, the fulfilment of needs is
only a by-product, never the driving force of the mechanism.
Valorisation is the aim: fulfilment of needs is at best a means,
since what has been produced must be sold. Even if it was
feasible, labour-managed value would still operate according
to valorisation. The bourgeois hardly control value: "people's
power" would not fare any better.

The company is the locus of capitalism: each industrial,
trading, or agricultural company operates as a rallying point
for a quantum of value looking for expansion. The enterprise
must make profits. Profitability has nothing to do with the
evil doing of a few "big" capitalists, and communism does
not mean getting rid of fat cigar smokers wearing top hats
at horse shows.[5] Old and new reformism always targets the
rich, yet what matters is not individual profits, however
outrageous they may be, but the constraint, the orientation
imposed upon production and society by a system which dictates what and how to produce and to consume.

This is why it is so difficult to draw a line between specu-
lative and productive investment. In capitalist logic, productive means *value* production, whether value comes out of a
Wolfsburg assembly line or a Wall Street trader's office. The
aim of production is not to satisfy human wants, nor provide

labour with jobs, nor to please the engineer's inventive mind, but to accumulate value. Of course this enables the bourgeois to amass fortunes, but only in so far as he fulfils his function. There is no point in contrasting the "real" economy that manufactures clothes with "parasitic" finance that plays with derivatives. The bottom line reality is to be read at the end of the financial statement that shows net income or loss.

5) A World of Companies

"It is important to emphasize the point that what determines value is not the time taken to produce a thing, but the minimum time it could possibly be produced in, and the minimum is ascertained by competition."[6]

Competition is the cornerstone of capitalism, the dynamic that makes it not only produce a lot more than other systems, but makes it the world-system where labour *productivity* is a priority. Each corporation meets its rivals on the market, each fights to corner the market.

Competition disjoints productive systems into autonomous centres which are rival poles, each seeking to increase its respective sum of value, which exists against the others. Soft and "fair" competition is not uncommon, but any firm will resort to cut-throat methods if it has to. Neither "corporate governance," nor "ethical guidelines," nor "democratic planning" can pacify economic warfare. The motive force of competition is not the freedom of individuals, nor even of the capitalists, but the freedom of capital: it lives by devouring itself. The form destroys its content to survive as a form. It destroys its material components (living labour and past labour) to survive as a sum of value valorising itself.

Each competing capital has a specific profit rate. But capitals move from one branch to another, looking for the best possible profit opportunity, for the most rewarding sector or niche. When this sector is saturated with capital, its profitability decreases and capitals are eventually transferred to another one. When CDs won the day, very few record companies kept mass-manufacturing vinyl. This unceasing dynamic process is modified, but not abolished, by the establishment of monopolies and oligopolies, which play a permanent war and peace game between themselves.

"Social Darwinism" expresses a world where one has to battle to sell *and to sell oneself*. Economic violence is complemented by armed State violence. Capitalist built-in tendencies combine with "push" political factors to make the world safe for war, and the social system that prides itself on its pacifying features makes us live between one impending conflict and the next.

6) Bureaucratic (or "State") Capitalism

Nothing changes so long as there exist production units each trying to increase its respective amount of value. If the State ("democratic," "workers'," "proletarian," etc.) takes all companies under its control, while keeping them as companies, either State enterprises obey the law of profit and value, and nothing changes; or they try to bend the rule, with some success . . . which cannot last for ever.

This is what happened to bureaucratic capitalism. In spite of "established" prices set by a State body, by the industrial sector, by the firm, or by some bargaining between the three, "socialist" firms could not go on unless they accumulated value at a socially acceptable rate. This rate was certainly not the same in Zamosc as in London. As in England, Polish firms were managed as separate units, with the difference that in Zamosc (unlike London) there was no private proprietor free to sell or buy a factory at will. Still, a Polish company manufacturing furniture did not just produce tables and sofas supposed to fulfil a function: it had to make the best profitable use of all the money that had been invested to produce these tables and sofas. "Value formation" mattered differently in Zamosc and London, but it did matter. No sofa was given free to the inhabitant of Zamosc for him to take home: just like the Londoner, he paid for his new sofa or went back home without.

Of course, the Polish State could subsidise sofas and sell them at too low a price, i.e. below production cost: that game could last a while . . . until value finally staked its claim. Russian and Polish planners kept bending the rules of profitability, but these rules asserted themselves in the end, through poor quality, shortages, waste, black market, purging of managers, etc. In England, a non-competitive furniture manufacturer would have gone bankrupt. In Poland, the State protected companies against bankruptcy. Yet no-one can fiddle the logic of valorisation for too long. One firm, ten firms, a thousand could be saved from closure, until one day it was the whole society that went bankrupt. If her Majesty's government had kept bailing out every unprofitable company from the early days of industrialisation, capitalism would now be defunct in Britain. The "law of value," viz. regulation by the social average time, functioned in very different ways in "bureaucratic" and in "market" capitalism, but it did apply to both.[7]

Value (de)formation was the inner weakness of the USSR, and this Achilles heel, as much as the war of economic attrition with the United States (the Russian State spent between one third and one half of its income on the military) caused the demise of bureaucratic capitalism.

7) Crisis

On the one hand, capital has socialised the world: all products tend to be the result of the activity of all humankind. On the other hand, our planet remains divided into competing corporations (backed by national States[8]), which try to produce what is profitable, and produce to sell as much as possible. Value accumulation leads to over-accumulation, and value production to over-production. Growth is *over*-growth. Each enterprise tries to valorise its capital in the best possible conditions. Each tends to produce more than the market can absorb and hopes that its competitors will be the only ones who suffer from overproduction. As business grows more concentrated and centralised, monopolies postpone over-production problems while further aggravating them until crisis re-adjusts supply to demand . . . only solvent demand, since capitalism only knows one way of circulating products: buying and selling.

We do not live simply in a world of commodities, but in a *capitalist* world which "presents itself as an immense accumulation of commodities," as written in *Das Kapital*'s first sentence. Capitalist crises are more than commodity crises: they link production to value in such a way that production is governed by value, as shown by comparing them with pre-capitalist crises.

Until the nineteenth century, a bad grain harvest would cause a decrease of agricultural production. The peasants bought fewer manufactured goods such as clothing or equipment, and industry found itself in trouble. Merchants speculated on corn and kept it in storage to drive prices up. Eventually there were famines here and there. The very existence of commodities and money is the condition for crises: there is a separation (materialised in time) between the two operations of buying and selling. From the standpoint of the merchant trying to increase his wealth, buying and selling corn are two distinct matters in time, the interval being determined by the amount and rate of his expected profit. In the interval between production and consumption, people starved: during the Irish famine of the 1840s, one million died while Ireland was a food net exporter. The mercantile system only acted as an aggravating circumstance in a crisis caused by climatic factors. The social context was pre-capitalist, or that of a weak capitalism, as in present-day China and Russia where bad harvests still have devastating effects on the economy and the people.[9]

Capitalist crisis, on the other hand, is the product of the forced union of value and production. Take a car maker. Competition forces him to raise productivity and get a maximum value output through a minimal input (cheapest possible raw materials, machinery, and labour). A crisis arises when accumulation does not go with a sufficient decrease in the costs of production. Thousands of cars may come off the assembly line every day, and even find buyers, but manufacturing and selling them does not valorise this capital enough compared to other car makers. So the company streamlines production, invests more, makes up profit loss with the number of cars sold, resorts to credit, mergers, government subsidies or tariffs, etc., eventually produces as if demand was to expand for ever, and loses more and more. Crises lie neither in the exhaustion of markets, nor in overgenerous pay rises, but in falling profits (to which workers' militancy contribute): as a sum of value, capital finds it increasingly hard to valorise itself at a socially acceptable rate.

Pre-capitalist crises originated from an unavoidable reality (wet winter and freezing, for instance) which mercantile relations only made worse. Modern crises have no such natural origin: their cause is social. All the elements of industrial activity are present—raw materials, machines, workers—and left to lie fallow. They are not just things, material objects: they only exist socially if value brings them to life. This phenomenon is not "industrial"; it does not come from technical requirements. It is a social relation: productive apparatus and social structure are ruled by mercantile logic.[10]

It is commonplace to bemoan the sad facts that office blocks are built more readily than lodgings for the homeless, that while hundreds of millions go hungry, food production is mainly promoted where it suits agro-business, or that the automotive industry remains a hyper-developed sector in spite of the damage it causes. This is crying out against the evils of a system as if we could only benefit from its virtues. The global network of enterprises—as centres of value which must yield a required profit rate—has become a power towering above us, and people's needs of all kinds (lodging, food, "culture") are subjected to valorisation and ultimately shaped by it.

In capitalism, *productive* designates what expands value, i.e. what produces either means of production, or means of livelihood for the proletarian, both accruing the sum of value. As a result, capital takes possession of science and technique: in the productive field, it orients research towards what will minimise labour cost; in the unproductive field, it stimulates management and marketing.

Thus mankind tends to be divided into three groups:

- productive workers, often physically destroyed by their work, by having their "life-time transformed into working-time," in the words of American worker Paul Romano in 1947;[11]
- unproductive workers, the vast majority of whom are only a source of waste;
- and the mass of non–wage earners, some of them in "rich" countries or areas, but most of them in less capitalist-developed "poor" countries. Since it has no means of livelihood because it is deprived of any means of production, a large part of the world's population has to sell its labour power in order to live . . . but it can't: capital only buys labour that brings in profit, so this labour power remains forcibly idle.[12]

The economic "take-off" of some formerly less-developed countries, like Brazil, is quite real, but can only be achieved through the partial or total destruction of former ways of life. The introduction of the commodity economy deprives poor peasants of their means of subsistence, leaves them landless or drives them to the misery of overcrowded towns. Only a minority is "lucky" enough to find a factory, shop, or office job, or to work as a servant; the rest is under-employed or unemployed.[13]

8) Proletariat and Revolution

Any revolution originates in material living conditions which have become unbearable. This also applies to the proletariat.

If one identifies *proletarian* with *factory worker* (or with manual labourer), or with the poor, one misses what is subversive in the proletarian condition. The proletariat is the negation of this society. It is not the collection of the poor, but of those who are dispossessed, "without reserves,"[14] who are nothing, have nothing to lose but their chains, and cannot liberate themselves without destroying the whole social order.

The proletariat is the dissolution of present society, because this society deprives the proletarians of nearly all its positive aspects: the proles only get their share of capitalist material, mental, and cultural wealth in its poorest aspects. All theories (bourgeois, fascist, Stalinist, Labourite, left-wing, or far-leftist) which somehow glorify and praise the proletariat as it is and claim for it the positive role of defending values and regenerating society, are anti-revolutionary. Enlightened bourgeois even admit the existence of class struggle, providing it never ends, in a self-perpetuating bargaining game between labour and capital, where the proletariat is reduced to the status of an element of capital, an indispensable wheel within an inevitable mechanism. The bourgeois does not mind the worker as long as he remains a partner.

Defining the proletariat has something but little to do with sociology. Indeed, most proles are low paid, and a lot work in production, yet their existence as proletarians derives not from being low-paid producers, but from being "cut off," alienated, with no control either over their lives or the outcome and meaning of what they have to do to earn a living. The proletariat therefore includes the unemployed and many housewives, since capitalism hires and fires the former, and utilises the labour of the latter to increase the total mass of extracted value. The proletariat is what reproduces value and can do away with a world based on value. Without the possibility of communism, theories of "the proletariat" would be tantamount to metaphysics. Our only vindication is that whenever it autonomously interrupted the running of society, the proletariat has repeatedly acted as negation of the existing order of things, has offered it no positive values or role, and has groped for something else.

The bourgeoisie, on the other hand, are ruling class not because they're rich and the rest of the population aren't. Being bourgeois brings them riches, not the other way round. They are ruling class because they control the economy—employees as well as machines. Individual ownership strictly speaking is only a form of class domination in particular variants of capitalism. Private property did not exist in State capitalism: the bureaucratic ruling class collectively owned the means of production.

Although a lot of proles work, the proletariat is not the working class, rather *the class of the critique of work.* It is the ever-present destruction of the old world . . . potentially: the potential only becomes real in moments of tension and upheaval. It only acts as the subversion of established society when it unifies and organises itself, not in order to become the dominant class like the bourgeoisie did, but in order to destroy the society of classes: when that prospect is achieved, there will be only one social agent: humankind. Till then, our historical terrain will remain one of clashing *class* interests.

Communist theory is not worker-centred or workplace-centred: it does not eulogise the working class, nor regards manual work as infinite bliss. It gives productive workers a decisive (but not exclusive) part because their place in production puts them in a better situation to revolutionise it. Only in this sense do "blue collar" (man *and* woman) workers keep a central role as initiators and precipitants, in so far as their social function enables them to carry out different tasks from others in an insurrection. Yet with the spread of unemployment, casual labour, longer schooling, training periods at any time of life, temp and part-time jobs, forced early retirement, and the odd mixture of welfare and workfare whereby people move out of misery into work and then again into poverty and moonlighting, when dole money sometimes equals low pay, it is getting harder to tell work from non-work.

We may well soon be entering a phase similar to the dissolution Marx's early writings referred to. In every period of intense historical disturbances (the 1840s as after 1917), the proletariat reflects the loosening of social boundaries (sections of both working and middle classes slip down the social ladder or fear they might) and the weakening of traditional values (culture is no longer a unifier). The conditions of life of the old society are already negated in those of the proles. Not hippies or punks, but modern capitalism makes a sham of the work ethic. Property, family, nation, morals, politics in the sense of periodic re-sharing and re-shuffling of power between quasi-similar bourgeois factions, all social props and pillars tend to decay as they are negated, delegitimised, "swamped" as Marx wrote, in the proletarian condition. In other words, the proletariat is not the working class, but

> a class with radical chains, a class of civil society which is not a class of civil society, an estate which is the dissolution of all estates, a sphere which has a universal character by its universal suffering and claims no particular right because no particular wrong, but wrong generally, is perpetuated against it; which can invoke no historical, but only human, title; . . . a sphere, finally, which cannot emancipate itself without emancipating itself from all other spheres of society and thereby emancipating all other spheres of society, which, in a word, is the complete loss of man and hence can win itself only through the complete re-winning of man.[15]

> Of all the classes that stand face to face with the bourgeoisie today, the proletariat alone is a really revolutionary class. The other classes decay and finally disappear in the face of modern industry; the proletariat is its special and essential product.[16]

If these two quotes do not contradict each other, the emphasis is undoubtedly different. The 1843 "radical humanist" or "universal class" approach morphed four or five years later into the "class analysis" of the *Communist Manifesto*. These quotes are but two among many, and not just in Marx's time: such theoretical ambiguity reflects the practical contradiction that the proletariat actually *is*:

If it was above all *working* class, how could it abolish work? How could a class primarily fighting another class (the bourgeois) defeat its enemy and *at the same time* get rid of all classes?

On the other hand, if the proletarians were just a couple of billion dispossessed people defined by what they are not, have not and do not, how could such an infinite but *entirely negative* mass achieve anything positive? Communisation is rejection and creation. Both.

Therefore proletarians are the wage-labour class, though this is often brought down to a wage-less condition. The definition has to be positive *and* negative: they are both *in* and *out of* this world. Only communist revolution will prove communist theory right, and solve the contradiction for good.

9) Communism as the End of Economy and Work

For the dispossessed masses, the capitalist socialisation of the world creates an entirely new reality. Unlike the slaves, serfs, or craftsmen of the past, the wage-labour (often wage-*less*, as we said) "immense majority" is potentially unified for collective action capable of overthrowing capitalism and creating a cooperative social life. Such is the crux of communist theory.

What Marx called capitalism's "historical role" was to create conditions which enable human beings (providing they make a revolution to that effect) to do without mediations that up to now have organised and imprisoned them. Value is one of those mediations: it materialises the social character of human activity. Value, concretised in money in all its forms, from the simplest (small change in your pocket) to the most sophisticated (credit lines on a trader's computer screen), results from the general character of labour, from the individual and social energy produced and consumed by labour. We can now dispense with an element external to social activities yet (up to now) necessary to connect and stimulate them. Communism does not reduce the components of social life to a common denominator (the average labour time contained in them): it compares utility to decide what to do and what to produce. Its material life is based on the confrontation and interplay of needs—which does not exclude conflicts and possibly some form of violence. Human beings will never be selfless angels, and why should they?

We can only approach social reality with words inherited from a few millennia of exploitation and deprivation. When we speak of *needs*, the term immediately conveys the idea of a lack, an absence, a deficiency. "Need" is what one wants but does not have, whether it is something obviously vital (food for the hungry) or deemed superfluous (a designer suit). It refers to an object or service as separate from me as production is cut off from consumption. Need is rarely understood as social, as something positive that connects me with others, me with the rest of the world, and me with the fulfilment of the need. Except if I am starving, my satisfaction in eating includes the fact that I have been longing for food. Providing one does not wait in vain, pleasure lies also in the waiting.

The natural urge to grow food, potatoes for instance, will be met through the birth of social links which will also result in vegetable gardening. The question is not how to grow potatoes because we have to eat. Rather, it is to imagine and invent a way to meet, to get and be together, that will include vegetable gardening and be productive of potatoes. Maybe potato growing will require more time than under capitalism, but that possibility will not be evaluated in terms of labour-time cost and saving.[17]

Communism is not an entirely different economy: it is the end of *the economy* as a separate and privileged domain on which everything else depends, and where work is—like money—the source of a universal love-hate relationship. Humankind produces and reproduces its conditions of existence. Ever since the disintegration of primitive communities, but in an extreme form under capitalism, the activity through which man appropriates his environment has taken the form of work—both an obligation and a compulsion. On the one hand, it is a curse, a constraint opposed to leisure and "true" enjoyable life. On the other, it is so pervasive that it often pre-empts the worker's capability for other activity outside working hours, and many proletarians feel at a loss in their "free time," or when they retire. Work is a blessing and a curse. With capital, production, i.e. production for valorisation, has become our master. It is a dictatorship of production relations over society. When one produces, one sacrifices one's life-time in order to enjoy life afterwards; this enjoyment is disconnected from the actual content of the work, which is a means of supporting one's life (workaholics are more numerous among taxation experts than street cleaners).

Communism dissolves production relations as separate and re-integrates them within the whole of social relations. The obligation of doing the same work for a lifetime, of being a manual or an intellectual worker, or of *forced* multi-tasking, disappears. Communism supports neither play against work, nor non-work against work. These limited and partial notions are capitalist mutilated realities. Activity as the production-reproduction of the conditions of life (material, affective, cultural, etc.) is the very nature of humanity, bearing in mind that "production" is a lot more than object-making: for instance, travelling produces ideas and experiences which transform people and contribute to inventions and new activities.

Some tasks will be taken in charge by everyone, and we can trust human inventiveness to come up with a wealth of new occupations. Automation probably will help. But believing in automation as the solution to the age-old malediction of work would be trying to address a social issue by technical means (actually, this is what capitalism pretends to be doing).

First, fully automated production (including huge computer networks) requires so much raw material and energy that overextending it would be wasting even more resources than contemporary industry does.

Secondly and more importantly, the human species collectively creates and transforms the means of its existence. If we received them from machines, we would be reduced to the status of a young child who is given toys without knowing where they come from: their manufactured origin does not even exist for him.

Neither does communism turn production into something perpetually pleasant and playful. Human life is effort and pleasure. Poetry-writing involves stress and pain. Learning another language implies a degree of exertion. Lots of things can be boring at times, vegetable gardening no exception, and communism will never fully abolish the difference between effort and enjoyment, creation and recreation. The all-leisure society and the push-button factory are capitalist utopias.

10) Communisation

In Marx's time and until much later, communist revolution was conceived as if its material preconditions were still to be created all over the world, and not just in "backward" countries like Russia or China: in the industrialised West as well. Nearly all Marxists—and a few anarchists—believed that when it took power, the working class would have to further develop the economy, in a different way from the bourgeois of course: it would reorient production in the interests of the masses, put the petit-bourgeois to work and generalise factory-type labour. In the best of schemes, this went along with worker management, equal pay and substantial reduction of working hours. But revolution did not come, and its German stronghold was crushed. Since then, such a programme has been fulfilled—over-fulfilled—by capitalist economic growth. The material basis of communism now exists. There is no longer any need to pack off clerks and shop-assistants to the shop floor, to turn *white* into *blue* collar: our problem will be to create a totally different "industry" . . . and to close quite a few factories. Compulsory labour is out of the question: what we want is *the abolition of work as such*, as an activity separate from the rest of life. For example, putting an end to garbage collection as a job some have to do for years, will be a lot more than job rotation: it will imply changes in the process and logic of garbage *creation* and disposal.

Underdeveloped countries—to use a capitalist phrase—will not have to go through industrialisation. In many parts of Asia, Africa, and Latin America, capital oppresses labour but has not subjugated it to what Marx called "real" submission: it dominates societies which it has not yet fully turned into money and wage-labour relationships. Old forms of social communal life still exist. Communism would regenerate a lot of them—as Marx expected the Russian peasant commune might do—with the help of some "Western" technology applied in a different way:

> If revolution comes at the opportune moment, if it con-
> centrates all its forces so as to allow the rural commune
> full scope, the latter will soon develop as an element of
> regeneration in Russian society and an element of superi-
> ority over the countries enslaved by the capitalist system.[18]

In many respects, "backward" areas may prove easier to communise than huge motorcar-adapted and screen-addicted "civilised" conurbations.

To pre-empt glib critique, let us add that communisation is of course *not instantaneous*: its effects will take time, at least a generation. But it will be *immediate*: it will proceed without the mediation of a "transition period" which would be neither capitalist nor non-capitalist. The process of living without value, work, and wage-labour will start in the early insurrec-tionary days, and then extend in depth and scope.

Communism is mankind's appropriation of its wealth, and implies an inevitable and complete transformation of this wealth. It is not a continuation of capitalism in a more rational, more efficient, and less unequal, less uncontrolled form. It does not take over the old material bases as it finds them: it overthrows them. We will not get rid of the "bad" side of capital (valorisation) while keeping the "good" side (produc-tion). Capital accumulates value and fixes it in the form of stored labour, past labour: nearly all present workplaces are geared to labour productivity and labour submission. (Most buildings too, schools particularly.) Communist revolution is a *dis*-accumulation. Communism is opposed to productiv-ism, and equally to the illusion of sustainable development within the existing economic framework. The official spokes-persons of ecology never voice a critique of the economy as value-measuring, they just want to keep money under control. Economy and ecology are incompatible.

Communism is not a set of measures to be put into prac-tice after the seizure of power. It is a movement which already exists, not as a mode of production (there can be no communist island within capitalist society), but as a tendency to community and solidarity never realised in this society: when it is implemented today, however innovative it can be, this tendency causes little else than marginal social experiments incapable of structural change. What they usually breed is more alternative lifestyles than new ways of life.[19]

Some past proletarian movements were able to bring society to a standstill, and waited for something to come out of this universal stoppage. Communisation, on the contrary, will circulate goods without money, open the gate isolating a factory from its neighbourhood, close down another factory where the work process is too alienating to be technically improved, put an end to battery farming, do away with school as a specialised place which cuts off learning from doing for fifteen-odd years, pull down walls that force people to imprison themselves in three-room family units—in short, it will tend to break partitions. Eventually, communism will not even know what *value* was.

Insurrection implies carrying out a historical mutation in the way we live, which includes how and what we produce. In the shifting sands of troubled times, the outcome is unpredictable, but the insurgents' ability to confront police and army guns and armoured cars will depend on the social content of their endeavour. To neutralise and overcome their enemies, the proletarians' main propelling force will be their communising ability.

> Modern strategy means the emancipation of the bourgeoisie and the peasantry: it is the military expression of that emancipation. The emancipation of the proletariat will also have a particular military expression and a new specific warfare. That is clear. We can even analyse such a strategy from the material conditions of the proletariat.[20]

Insurrection cleaves the normal course of events and opens up make-or-break times. Up to now, insurgents have hardly ever reached the tipping point where creating an altogether new society could coincide with a corresponding armed action. In its culminating moments, for instance in Germany between 1919 and 1921, the proletariat never reached a communisation stage. Whereas the bourgeoisie resorted to its "natural" weapon—the economy—by dividing the working class through unemployment, the proletariat was unable to reply on the same scale by means of its blocking power over society. Though it went as far as to create a Red Army in the Ruhr in 1920, its military "offensive" remained socially defensive: the insurgents did not transform what they had taken control of. They did not raise the stakes by using the destructive-constructive "weapon" which their social function gives them.[21]

In a very different context, when some riots in the United States re-appropriated goods, they remained on the level of consumption and distribution. Rioters were attacking *commodity*, not *capital*.[22] Communisation will deal with the heart of the matter: value production. But the insurgents will only use this instrument if they transform it at the same time. Such a process can only take place on a worldwide scale, and first of all in several countries where social contradictions are more acute, which means communisation is more likely to be initiated in Western Europe, North America, and Japan.[23]

The question is not the seizure of power by the workers. It is absurd to advocate the rule of the working class as it is now: a partner in the valorisation mechanism, and a subjected partner.[24] Under the dominion of wage-labour and company, worker management is just capable of moderating the dictates of capital. The dictatorship of the existing working class cannot be anything but the dictatorship of its representatives, i.e. the leaders of the unions and workers' parties. This is the programme of the democratic left.

Theories of "workers' government" or "workers' power" only propose alternative solutions to the crisis of capital. Revolution transforms society, i.e. relations among people, and between people and their means of life. Organisational problems and "leaders" are secondary: they depend on what the revolution achieves. This applies as much to the start of the communist revolution as to the functioning of the society which arises out of it. Revolution will not happen on the day when 51 percent of the workers become revolutionary; and it will not begin by setting up a decision-making apparatus. Management and leadership dilemma are typical capitalist obsessions. The organisational form of the communist revolution, as of any social movement, hinges on its substance and development. The way revolution gets organised, constitutes itself and acts, results from the tasks it performs.

11) States and How to Get Rid of Them

Marx's early works suggested a *critique of politics*, and opposed "political" to "social" revolution: the former rearranges links between individuals and groups without much change in what they actually do; the latter acts upon how people reproduce their means of existence, their way of life, their real condition, at the same time transforming how they relate to each other.[25]

One of our first spontaneous rebellious gestures is to revolt against control over our lives from above, by a teacher, a boss, a policeman, a social worker, a union leader, a statesman . . . Then politics walks in and reduces aspirations and desires to a problem of power—be it handed to a party, or shared by everyone. But what we really lack is the power to produce our life. A world where all electricity comes to us from mammoth (coal, fuel-oil, or nuclear) power stations, will always remain out of our reach. Only the political mind thinks revolution is primarily a question of power seizure or redistribution.

Understanding this critique of politics is essential to grasp the issue of the State.

We described value as an element external to social activities and up to now necessary to connect and stimulate them.

In a similar way, the State was born out of human beings' inability to manage their lives. It is the unity—symbolic and material—of the disunited: some *social contract* has to be agreed upon. As soon as proletarians start appropriating their means of existence, this mediation begins to lose its function, but destroying it is not an automatic process. It will not disappear little by little as the non-mercantile sphere gets bigger and bigger. Actually, such a sphere would be vulnerable if it let the central governmental machinery go on, as in Spain 1936–37. No State structure will wither away on its own.

Communising is therefore more than adding piecemeal actions. Capital will be sapped by general subversion through which people take their relationships with the world into their own hands. But nothing decisive will be achieved as long as the State retains its hold on the essential. Society is not simply a capillary network: relationships are centralised in a force which concentrates the power to preserve this society. Capitalism would be too happy to see us change our lives locally while it carries on globally. Because it is a central force, the State has to be demolished by central action. Because its power base is ubiquitous, it must be extinguished everywhere. Communisation will combine both dimensions . . . or fail. The communist movement is *anti*-political, not *a*-political.

Writing and reading about violence and even more so armed violence is easy, and carries the risk of mistaking the pen for a sword. All the same, no reflection on revolution can evade the issue. Our purpose is neither to prepare for a revamped Red Army, nor for worker militia modelled on the 1936 Spanish experience, where the participants received *pay*: traditional military they were not, yet like soldiers they were given *money* to live on. This alone showed the absence of communisation.

In any deep historical change, the nature, extent, degree, and control of violence depends on what is changed, by whom and how.

Since the communisation of society would begin at once and gradually involve more and more people, its inevitable violence would be different from what Marx or Rosa Luxemburg could imagine. The proletarians will be able to make the bourgeoisie and the State, i.e. the political props of capitalist economy, utterly useless and ultimately defenceless,

by undermining the sources of their power. The bourgeoisie is aware of it: modern States are steeling themselves for
"low-intensity operations," which imply a lot more than police
work, and include population and resource control. Of course
counter-revolution has never been *only* military and political,
but its social dimension is now a condition of the rest. In 1972,
though it dealt mostly with wars in the Third World, Michael
Klare's *War Without End: American Planning for the Next Vietnams*
provided useful insights into the strategy of the big capitalist
States preparing for civil war on their own soil. If we considered the problem from a purely material point of view, the
State's superiority would be outstanding: guns against tanks.
Our hope resides in a subversion so general and yet so coherent that the State will be confronted by us everywhere, and
its energy source depleted.

Communist revolution "destroys" less than it deprives
counter-forces by draining them of their function. The
Bolsheviks did the opposite: they got rid of the bourgeois, left
the basics of capitalism survive, and ended up fulfilling the
capitalist function in the place of the bourgeois. Lenin and
his party started 1917 as political activists, became efficient
soldiers, and after winning the war turned into managers.

On the contrary, as communisation is immediate (in the
sense defined in the previous section), it does not separate *ends*
from *means*: it does not aim at political power, for instance by
creating a stronger military force than the State's army: it
aims at the power of transforming social relations, which
include the self-transformation of the insurgents themselves.

12) Democracy?

Communism may be called "democratic" if democracy means
that everyone has a say in the running of society, but this will
not be so because of people's ability and desire to manage
society, or because we would all be educated enough to master
the art of sound administration.

Our problem is not to find how to take truly common
decisions about what we do, but *to do* what can be decided

upon in common. A Taylorised factory will never come under the management of its personnel. Neither will a farm based on value productivity. A General Motors plant, a nuclear power station, Harvard University or the BBC will never operate democratically. A company or an institution run like a business accepts no leadership but that which allows it to valorise itself. The enterprise manages its managers, and capitalists are the officials of capital. The elimination of the limits of the company, the destruction of the commodity relation which compels every individual to treat others as a means to earn his living, here are the main conditions for self-organisation. Instead of making management a priority, communism will regard administration as an activity among others.

> Democracy is a contradiction in terms, a lie and indeed sheer hypocrisy. . . . This applies to all forms of government. Political freedom is a farce and the worst possible slavery; such a fictitious freedom is the worst enslavement. So is political equality: this is why democracy must be torn to pieces as well as any other form of government. Such a hypocritical form cannot go on. Its inherent contradiction must be exposed in broad daylight: either it means true slavery, which implies open despotism; or it means real freedom and real equality, which implies communism.[26]

Most utopian socialists looked for some pre-ordained external factor which would compel individuals to live in harmonious unity. Despite their visionary foresight, imaginary communities often resort to strict planning and "soft" despotism. To avoid chaos and exploitation, utopians devised schemes to organise social life in advance. Others, from an anarchist standpoint, refuse any institution and want society to be a permanent re-creation. But the problem lies elsewhere: only non-mercantile non-productivity relations can make harmony among individuals both possible and necessary. "Fair" and "efficient" links depend on the way we associate to do something together, be it planting fruit trees or having a

party. Then individuals can fulfil their needs, through participation in the functioning of the group, without being mere
tools of the group. That being said, harmony does not exclude
the likelihood of conflicts.

To avoid discussing in the abstract, let us wander if the
democratic principle applies in social life. The 1986 French
railway strike was to a large extent (at any rate, a lot more
than is commonly the case) self-organised by the rank and
file. At Paris-Nord, a train engine drivers' meeting had just
voted against blocking the tracks to prevent trains from
running. Suddenly the strikers saw a train come out of the
station, driven by middle managers under police protection:
they rushed to the tracks to stop it, undoing by spontaneous
action hours of democratic deliberation.

What does this (and hundreds of similar instances)
prove? Certainly not that any rash initiative going against
collective decision is positive. It simply reminds us that *collective* is not synonymous with what is usually often referred
to as democracy: a deliberation process organised according
to a set of pre-planned rules.

Communism is of course the movement of a vast majority at long last able to take actions into their own hands. To
that extent, communism is "democratic," but it does not
uphold democracy as a principle. Politicians, bosses, and
bureaucrats take advantage either of a minority or a majority
when it suits them: so does the proletariat. Workers' militancy
often stems from a handful. Communism is neither the rule
of the most numerous, nor of the wise few. To debate or start
acting, people obviously have to gather somewhere, and such
common ground has been called a soviet, committee, council,
shura, etc. The means turns into an end, however, when the
moment and machinery of decision-making prevail over
action. This separation is the essence of parliamentarianism.

True, people must decide for themselves and, at some
point or other, this requires a "discursive" time and space.
But any decision, revolutionary or not, depends on what has
happened before and what *is still going on* outside the formal

deciding structure. Whoever organises the meeting sets the agenda; whoever asks the question determines the answer; whoever calls the vote often carries the decision. Revolution does not put forward a different form of organisation, but a different solution from that of capital and reformism. As principles, democracy and dictatorship are equally wrong: they isolate a special and seemingly privileged moment. Communism is neither democratic nor dictatorial.

The essence—and limit—of political thought is to wonder *how to organise* people's lives, instead of considering first *what* those to-be-organised people *do*.

Communism is not a question of inventing the government or self-government best suited to the social reorganisation we want. It is not a matter of institutions, but of activity.

What members of society have in common or not depends on what they are *doing* together. When they lose mastery over the material basis of their conditions of existence, they lose their mastery over the running of their personal and group life.

In sum, communisation will deprioritise the power question, by stressing the *nature of the change*: revolution will be born out of a common refusal to submit, out of the hope of getting to a point of no return where people transform themselves and gain a sense of their own power as they transform reality.[27]

13) Break on through (to the Other Side)

The world of commodities and value is activated by us, yet it lives a life of its own, it has constituted itself into an autonomous force, and the world at large has to submit to its laws. Communism challenges this submission and has opposed it since the early days of capitalism, so far with no chance of success.

The communist revolution is the continuation as well as the surpassing of present social movements. Communism will grow out of struggles, out of real interest and desires which are now already trying to assert themselves, and cannot be satisfied because the present situation forbids it. Today numerous communist gestures and attitudes express more than a refusal of the present world: they express an attempt to get to a new one. Whenever they succeed, they are confined to a social fringe, and tolerated as long as they do not antagonise wage-labour and State: otherwise, they are "recuperated," stifled or suppressed. Public opinion only sees their limits, only the tendency and not its possible development, and "extremism" or "alternativism" always present these limits as the true aims of the movement. In the refusal of assembly-line work, in the struggles of squatters, the communist perspective is present as the social energy spent to create "something else," not to escape the modern world, but to transform it. In such conflicts people spontaneously try to appropriate goods, or even make goods and invent new types of goods, against the logic of value exchange, and this process helps the participants to change themselves in the event.

However, that "something else" is present only potentially in these actions, whatever the people involved think and want, and whatever activists and theorists may do and say. Communisation is not embryonic in any strike, riot, or looting, and trying to radicalise them is tantamount to trying to change something into what it cannot be *now*. The only possible "autonomous" spaces in this society are those allowed by capital and State, therefore politically harmless. When the social experimenter sneaks into the cracks of conformity, the crack closes in on him. Revolution is fun (besides being other things): not all fun is revolutionary. The course of history is neither piecemeal nor gradual: revolution is a cut, a break-through. "The gate is straight, deep and wide," but we still have to cross the gate to get to the other side.

CHAPTER 2

■ THE CLASS STRUGGLE AND ITS MOST CHARACTERISTIC ASPECTS IN RECENT YEARS

By François Martin*

This essay was started soon after May '68 and completed in 1972. François Martin had worked years before in an Algerian shoemaking factory under (State-controlled) "self-management," where he experienced how a spontaneous desire to get a grip on one's fate could end in self-exploitation. Apart from very few minor corrections, his text has been left as it was: we have only integrated Martin's own notes within the text to distinguish them from ours.

If this text was written today, historical data would be different. Though it still retains strongholds, the French CP has declined, partly through de-industrialisation of traditional working class areas. Besides, one can no longer speak of "Stalinism." CPs were Stalinist not out of love for Russia, but because State capitalism was a possible solution for capital . . . usually with Red Army troops around. With the downfall of the USSR, this backward form of capitalism has outlived its usefulness, and CPs have evolved into proponents of radical reforms, or simply disbanded. The traditionally adaptable Italian CP had already gone this way for quite a while before the bulk of the party disappeared in a centre-left party. After protected resistance, the die-hard French CP is now following suit. The sixty-year-old sinister Stalinist farce has been sent to the dustbins of history, alas

---

* François Martin was the pen name of François Cerutti, who recently published a book on that part of his life: *D'Alger à Mai 68. Mes années de révolution* (Paris: Spartacus, 2010).

not by the proletariat, but by the overwhelming drive of commodities. "If you want a picture of the future, imagine a boot stamping on
a human face," Orwell wrote in 1984. Sometimes, the credit card is
mightier than the jackboot.

More importantly, such an essay today would take into account
the worker defeat in the West after the 1970s, and the unrest and
struggles that have recently swelled, especially but not only in Asia.
Our *Postlude* will briefly examine these changes.

(G.D., 2013)

The original purpose of this text was to try to show the fundamental reasons why the revolutionary movement of the
first half of the century took various forms (parties, trade and
industrial unions, workers' councils) which now not only
belong to the past, but also hinder the re-formation of the
revolutionary movement. But only part of the project was
carried out. This task still has to be realised. But it would be a
mistake to wait for a complete theoretical construction before
moving on. The following text gives certain elements which
are useful for an understanding of new forms of the communist "party." Recent events (mainly strikes in the United
States, in Britain, in France, and Italy) clearly show that we
are entering a new historical period. For example, the French
Communist Party (PCF) still dominates the working class, but
it is under strong attack. While for a long period of time the
revolutionary movement's opposition to capital was deflected
by the PCF, today this mediation tends to disappear: the opposition between workers and capitalism is going to assert itself
more and more directly, and on the level of real facts and
actions, as opposed to the situation when the ideology of the
PCF was prominent among workers and the revolutionary
movement had to fight against the PCF mainly on a theoretical level.

Today revolutionaries will be forced to oppose capital
practically. This is why new theoretical tasks are necessary.
It is not enough to agree on the level of ideas; one must take
positive action, and first of all intervene in present struggles

to support one's views. Communists do not have to build a separate party from the one which asserts itself in practice in our society; yet they will increasingly have to support their positions so that the real movement does not waste its time in useless and false struggles. Organic links (theoretical work for practical activity) will have to be established among those who think we are moving towards a conflict between the proletariat and capital. The present text tries to determine how the communist movement is going to reappear, and to define the tasks of the communists.

1) May 1968, France

The general strike of May 1968 was one of the biggest strikes in capitalist history. Yet it is probably the first time in contemporary society that such a powerful working class movement did not create for itself organs capable of expressing it. More than four years of workers' struggles prove this fact. Nowhere can we see organisations going beyond a local and temporary contact. Unions and parties have been able to step into this void and negotiate with the bosses and the State. In 1968 a number of short-lived Action Committees were the only form of workers' organisation which acted outside the unions and the parties; the Action Committees opposed what they felt to be treason on the part of the unions.

Either at the beginning of the strike, or in the process of the sit-downs, or later, in the struggle against the resumption of work, many thousands of workers organised themselves in one way or another outside and against the will of the unions. But in every case these workers' organisations fizzled out with the end of the movement and did not turn into a new type of organisation.

The only exception was the "Inter-Enterprise" Committee, which had existed since the beginning of the strike at the Censier building of the "Faculté des Lettres" in Paris. It gathered together workers—individuals and groups—from several dozen factories in the Paris area. Its function was to coordinate actions against the undermining of the strike by the

PCF-controlled union, the CGT. It was in fact the only workers' organ which in practice went beyond the narrow limits of the factory by putting into practice the solidarity between workers from different firms. As is the case with all revolutionary activities of the proletariat, this Committee did not publicise its action.[1]

The Committee continued to organise meetings after the strike and disappeared after its members realised its uselessness. Of course the hundreds of workers who had taken part in its activity soon stopped coming to its meetings. Many of them continued seeing each other. But while the purpose of the Committee during the strike had been to strengthen the fight against union and party manoeuvres, it later turned into a discussion group studying the results of the strike and trying to learn its lessons for the future. These discussions often dealt with communism and its importance.

This Committee gathered a minority. Yet its daily "general assemblies" at Censier, as well as its smaller meetings, allowed several thousand workers to meet. It remained limited to the Paris area. We have heard of no such experiment in other regions, organised outside all unions (including "left-wing" unions: the town of Nantes, in the west of France, was more or less taken over by the unions during the strike).

One must add that a handful of people sharing communist ideas (a dozen at most) were deeply involved in its action and functioning. The result of this was to limit the influence of the CGT, the Trotskyists, and the Maoists, to a minimum. The fact that the Committee was outside all traditional union and party organisations, including the extremist ones, and that it tried to go beyond the limit of the factory, foreshadowed what has been happening since 1968. Its disappearance after the fulfilment of its tasks also foreshadowed the fading away of organisations that have appeared since then, in the most characteristic struggles of recent years.

This shows the great difference between the present situation and what happened in the 1930s. In 1936, in France, the working class fought behind the "workers'" organisations and for the reforms they professed. So the forty-hour week and two weeks of paid vacation were regarded as a real victory of the workers, whose essential demand was to get the same conditions and position as salaried groups. These demands were imposed on the ruling class. Today the working class is not asking for the improvement of its conditions of life. The reform programmes presented by unions and parties closely resemble those put forward by the State. It was De Gaulle who proposed "participation" as a remedy for what he called the "mechanical" society.

It seems that only a fraction of the ruling class realised the extent of the crisis, which it called a "crisis of civilisation" (André Malraux). Since then all organisations, all unions and parties, without any exceptions, rallied to the great reform programme in one way or another. The PCF itself includes "*real* participation" in its governmental programme. The other large union, the CFDT, advocates self-management, which is also supported by ultra-left groups who are in favour of "workers' councils." The Trotskyists propose "workers' control" as a minimum programme for a "workers' government."

What lies at the heart of all this concern is an attempt to end the separation between the worker and the product of his work. This is an expression of a "utopian" view of capital, and has nothing to do with communism. The capitalist "utopia" tries to do away with the bad side of exploitation. The communist movement cannot express itself in a formal criticism of capital. It does not aim to change the conditions of work, but the function of work: it wants to replace the production of exchange values with the production of use values. Whereas unions and parties carry on their debates within the context of one and the same programme, the programme of capital, the proletariat has a non-constructive attitude. Apart from its practical political activities, it does not "participate" in the debate organised about its case. It does not try to do theoretical research about its own tasks. This is the time of the great silence of the proletariat. The paradox is that the ruling class tries to express the aspirations of the workers, in its own way.

A fraction of the ruling class understands that the present conditions of appropriation of surplus-value are a hindrance to the total functioning of the economy. Its perspective is to share the cake, hoping that a working class "profiting" from capital and "participating" in it will produce more surplus-value. We are reaching the stage when capital dreams of its own survival, as proved by the 1972 MIT–Club of Rome report on *The Limits to Growth*. To achieve this survival, it would have to get rid of its own parasitical sectors, i.e. the fractions of capital which no longer produce enough surplus-value.

Whereas in 1936 the workers tried to reach the same level as other sectors of society, nowadays capital itself imposes on the privileged salaried sectors the same general conditions of life as those of the workers. The concept of "participation" (De Gaulle's phrase for what others call *class collaboration*) implies equality in the face of exploitation imposed by the needs of value formation. Thus participation is a "socialism" of misery. Capitalism must reduce the enormous cost of the sectors which are necessary to its survival but which do not directly produce value.

In the course of their struggles workers realise that the possibility of improving their material conditions is limited and on the whole already planned by capital. The working class can no longer intervene on the basis of a programme which would really alter its living conditions within capital-ism. The great workers' struggles of the first half of the century, struggles for the eight-hour day, the forty-hour week, paid holidays, industrial unionism, job security, showed that the relationship between the working class and capital allowed the workers a certain range of "capitalist" action. Nowadays capital itself imposes the reforms and generalises the equal-ity of all in the face of wage-labour. Therefore no important section of the working class is willing to fight for intermediate objectives as was the case at the beginning of the century or in the 1930s. But it should also be obvious that as long as the communist perspective is not clear there can be no formation of workers' organisations on a communist basis. This is not to say that the communist objectives will suddenly become clear to everybody. The fact that the working class is the only class which produces surplus-value is what places it at the centre of the crisis of value, i.e. at the very heart of the crisis of capitalism, and forces it to destroy all other classes as such, and to form the organs of its self-destruction as a part of capital, as a class within capitalism. The communist organisation will only appear in the practical process of destruction of the bourgeois economy, and in the creation of a human community without exchange.

The communist movement has asserted itself continually since the very beginning of capitalism. This is why capital is forced to maintain constant surveillance and continual violence over everything dangerous to its normal functioning. Ever since the secret conspiracy of Babeuf in 1795, the workers' movement has experienced increasingly violent and longer struggles, which have shown capitalism to be, not the culmination of humanity, but its negation.

Although the May '68 strike had hardly any immediate positive results, its real strength was that it did not give birth to durable illusions. The May "failure" is the failure of reformism, and the end of reformism breeds a struggle on a totally different level, a struggle against capital itself, not against its effects. In 1968 everyone was thinking of some "other" society. What people said rarely went beyond the notion of general self-management. Apart from the communist struggle which can develop only if the centre, the class which produces surplus-value, leads it, other classes can only act and think within the capitalist sphere, and their expression can only be that of capital—even of capital reforming itself. Yet behind these partial criticisms and alienated expressions we can see the beginning of the crisis of value which is characteristic of the historical period we are now entering.

These ideas do not come from nowhere; they always appear because the symptoms of a real human community exist emotionally in every one of us. Whenever the false community of wage-labour is questioned, there appears a tendency towards a form of social life in which relationships are no longer mediated by the needs of capital.

Since May '68, the activity of the communist movement has tended to be increasingly concrete.

2) Strikes and Workers' Struggles Since 1968

Whereas in the years after World War II strikes—even important ones—were kept under control and were not followed by constant political and monetary crises, the past few years have seen a renewal of industrial riots and even insurrections in France, Italy, Britain, Belgium, West Germany, Sweden, Denmark, Spain, Portugal, Switzerland. In Poland the workers attacked the headquarters of the CP while singing "The Internationale". The process was the same in nearly every case. A minority starts a movement with its own objectives; soon the movement spreads to other categories of workers in the same firm; people get organised (strike pickets, workers' committees in the shops, on the assembly lines); the unions manage to be the only ones capable of negotiating with the management; they finally get the workers to resume work, after proposing unitary slogans which no one likes but everyone accepts because of the inability to formulate anything else. The only movement which went beyond the stage of the strike as it now exists was the movement of riots and strikes in Poland in December 1970–January 1971.

What happened in a brutal way in Poland exists only as a tendency in the rest of the industrial world. In Poland there is no mechanism of "countervailing" power capable of keeping social crises in check. The ruling class had to attack the working class directly in order to maintain the process of value formation in normal conditions. The Polish events prove that the crisis of value tends to spread to all industrial areas, and demonstrate the behaviour of the working class as the centre of such a crisis.

The origin of the movement was the need to defend the average selling price of labour power. But the movement found itself immediately on another field: it had to face capitalist society itself. At once the workers were forced to attack the organs of oppression. Party and union officials were assaulted and the party building was stormed. In some towns the railway stations were guarded in case they might be used to bring troops. The movement was strong enough to give itself an organ of negotiation: a workers' committee for the town. The very fact that Edward Gierek had to go to the shipyards in person must be regarded as a victory of the working class as a whole.[2] A year later Fidel Castro had to go to Chile in person to ask the tin miners to cooperate with the ("socialist") government. In Poland the workers did not send delegates to the central power to propose their demands: the government had to come to the workers to negotiate . . . the inevitable surrender of the workers.

Facing the violence of the State, the working class formed its own organs of violence. No leaders had anticipated the organisation of the revolt: it was the product of the nature of the society the revolt tried to destroy. Yet leaders (the workers' committee for the town) only appeared after the movement had reached the highest point which the situation allowed. The negotiation organ is an expression of nothing more than the realisation by both sides that there is only one solution left. The characteristic of such a negotiation organ is that it implies no delegation of power. It rather represents the outer limit of a movement which cannot go beyond negotiation in the present situation. Reforms, once again, are proposed by capital, whereas the working class expresses itself in practical refusal; it must accept the proposals of the central power so long as its practical activity is not yet strong enough to destroy the basis of that power.

Workers' struggles tend to directly oppose their own dictatorship to that of capital, to organise on a different basis from that of capital, and thus to pose the question of the transformation of society by acts. When the existing conditions are unfavourable to a general attack, or when this attack fails, the forms of dictatorship disintegrate, capital triumphs again, reorganises the working class according to its logic, diverts the violence from its original aims, and separates the formal aspect of the struggle from its real content. We must get rid of the old opposition between "dictatorship" and "democracy." To the proletariat, "democracy" does not mean organising itself as a parliament in the bourgeois way; for it, "democracy" is an act of violence by means of which it destroys all the social forces which prevent it from expressing itself and maintain it as a class within capitalism. "Democracy" cannot be anything but a dictatorship. This is visible in every strike: the form of its destruction is precisely "democracy." As soon as there is a separation between a decision-making organ and an action organ, the movement is no longer in the offensive phase: it is being diverted to the ground of capital. Opposing workers' "democracy" to the union's "bureaucracy" means attacking a superficial aspect and hiding the real content of workers' struggles, which have a totally different basis. Democracy is now the slogan of capital: it proposes the self-management of one's own negation. All those who accept this programme spread the illusion that society can be changed by a general discussion followed by a vote (formal or informal) which would decide what is to be done. By maintaining the separation between decision and action, capital tries to maintain the existence of classes. If one criticises such a separation only from a formal point of view, without going to its roots, one merely perpetuates the division. It is hard to imagine a revolution which begins when voters raise their hands. Revolution is an act of violence, a process through which social relations are transformed.

We will not try to give a description of the strikes which have taken place since 1968. Though a large number of books and pamphlets have been written about them, we still lack too much information. We would only like to see what they have in common, and in what way they are the sign of a period in which communist prospects will appear more and more concretely.

We do not divide industrial society into different sectors—"developing" and "backward." It is true that some differences can be observed, but these can no longer hide from us the nature of the strikes, in which one cannot see real differences between "vanguard" and "rearguard" struggles. The process of the strikes is less and less determined by local factors, and more and more by the international conditions of capitalism. Thus the Polish strikes and riots were the product of an international context; the relationship between East and West was at the root of these events where people sang "The Internationale" and not the national anthem. Western and Eastern capital have a common interest in securing the exploitation of their respective workers. And the relatively under-developed "socialist" capitalisms must maintain a strict capitalist efficiency to be able to compete with their more modern Western neighbours.

The communist struggle starts in a given place, but its existence does not depend on purely local factors. It does not act according to the limits of its original birthplace. Local factors become secondary to the objectives of the movement. As soon as a struggle limits itself to local conditions, it is immediately swallowed up by capitalism. The level reached by workers' struggles is not determined by local factors, but by the global situation of capitalism. As soon as the class which concentrates in itself the revolutionary interests of society rises, it immediately finds, in its situation, and without any mediation, the content and object of its revolutionary activity: to crush its enemies and take the decisions imposed by the needs of the struggle; the consequences of its own actions force it to move further.

We shall not deal with all strikes here. There is still a capitalist society in which the working class is just a class of capitalism, a part of capital, when it is not revolutionary. Party and union machines still manage to control and lead considerable sections of the working class for the sake of capitalist objectives, such as the right to retire at sixty in France.[3] General elections and many strikes are organised by unions for limited demands. However, it is increasingly obvious that in most large strikes the initiative does not come from the unions, and these are the strikes we are talking about here. Industrial society has not been divided into sectors, nor has the working class been divided up into the young, the old, the natives, the immigrants, the foreigners, the skilled, and the unskilled. We do not oppose all sociological descriptions; these can be useful, but they are not our aim here.

We shall try to study how the proletariat breaks away from capitalist society. Such a process has a definite centre. We do not accept the sociological view of the working class because we do not analyse the working class from a static point of view, but in terms of its opposition to value. The rupture from capital abolishes exchange value, i.e. the existence of labour as a commodity. The centre of this movement, and therefore its leadership, must be the part of society which produces value. Otherwise it would mean that exchange value no longer exists, and that we are already beyond the capitalist stage. Actually the profound meaning of the essential movement is partially hidden by the struggles on the periphery, on the outskirts of the production of value. This was the case in May 1968, when students masked the real struggle, which took place elsewhere.

In fact the struggles on the outskirts (the new middle classes) are only a sign of a much deeper crisis which appearances still hide from us. The renewal of the crisis of value implies, for capital, the need to rationalise, and therefore to attack, the backward sectors which are least capable of protecting themselves; this increases unemployment and the number of those who have no reserves. But their intervention must not make one forget the essential role played by production workers in destroying exchange value.

3) The Two Most Characteristic Aspects of the Strikes

On one hand, the initiative of the strike comes from self-organised workers; on the other, the initiative to end the strike comes from the fraction of the workers organised in unions. These initiatives are contradictory since they express two movements which are opposed to one another. Nothing is more alien to a strike than its end. The end of a strike is a moment of endless talks when the notion of reality is overcome by illusions; many meetings are organised where union officials have a monopoly of speech; general assemblies attract fewer and fewer people and finally vote to resume work. The end of a strike is a time when the working class again falls under the control of capital, is again reduced to atoms, individual components, destroyed as a class capable of opposing capital. The end of a strike means negotiation, the control of the movement, or what is left of it, by "responsible" organisations, the unions. The beginning of a strike means just the opposite: then the action of the working class has nothing to do with formalism. All those who do not support the movement are pushed aside, whether they are executives, foremen, workers, managers, shop stewards, or union officials. Managers are locked up, union buildings attacked by thousands of workers, depending on local conditions. During the strike in Limbourg (Belgium, Winter 1970), the union headquarters were stormed by the workers. Everything acting as a hindrance to the movement tends to be destroyed. There is no place for "democracy": on the contrary, everything is obvious, and all enemies must be defeated without wasting time on discussions. A considerable amount of energy appears during the offensive phase, and it seems that nothing is able to stop it.

At this stage we cannot avoid stating an obvious fact: the energy at the beginning of the strike seems to disappear totally by the time of the negotiations. What is more important, this energy seems to have no relation to the official reasons given for the strike. If several dozens of men bring about a strike of thousands of workers on the basis of their own demands, they do not succeed just because of some sort of solidarity, but because of an immediate community in practice. We must add the most important point, that the movement does not put forward any particular demand. The question the proletariat will ask in practice is already present in its silence. In its own movements the proletariat does not put forward any particular demand: this is why these movements are the first communist activities in our time.

What is important in the process of breaking away from capitalism is that the working class no longer asks for partial and particular reforms. Thus the working class ceases to be a class, since it does not defend its particular class interests. This process is different according to the conditions. The movement which went the farthest, in Poland, showed that the first step of the process is the disintegration of the capitalist organs of repression within the working class (mainly the unions); the working class must next organise to protect itself against the organs of repression outside the working class (armed forces, police, militia), and start destroying them.

The specific conditions in Poland, where the unions are part of the State apparatus, forced the working class to make no distinction between the unions and the State, since there was none.[4] The fusion between unions and State only made obvious an evolution which does not appear as clearly in other countries, such as France and Italy. In many cases the unions still play the role of a buffer between the workers and the State. But a radical struggle will increasingly attack the unions and the sections of the working class dominated by the unions. The time is gone when workers form unions to defend their qualifications and their right to work.

The conditions of modern society compel the working class not to put forward any particular demand. The only community organised and tolerated by capital is the community of wage-labour: capital tends to forbid everything else. Capital now dominates the totality of the relations men have with one another. It becomes increasingly obvious that every partial struggle which is limited to a particular relation is forced to insert itself into a general struggle against the entire system of relations among people: capital. Otherwise it is integrated or destroyed.[5]

In a strike of the Paris bus and subway workers (RATP) at the end of 1971, the resolute attitude of the subway drivers turned the strike into a movement quite different from the strike of one particular category of workers. The content of the movement does not depend on what people think. The attitude of the drivers transformed their relation to the management of the RATP and the unions, and clearly revealed the true nature of the conflict. The State itself had to intervene to force the drivers back under the pressure of the unions. Whether the drivers believed it or not, the strike was no longer theirs; it had turned into a public trial where the unions were officially recognised as necessary organs of coercion against the workers, organs charged with the task of restoring the normal order of things. It is impossible to understand the importance of the "silence" of the working class unless one first understands the powerful development of capitalism until now. It is nowadays considered normal that the end of strikes should be controlled by unions. This does not imply any weakness on the part of the revolutionary movement. On the contrary, in a situation which does not allow partial demands to be achieved, it is normal that no organ should be created to end the strike. Thus we do not see the creation of workers' organisations gathering fractions of the working class outside the unions on a programme of specific demands. Sometimes workers' groups are formed during the struggle, and they oppose their demands to those of the unions, but their chances are destroyed by the situation itself, which does not allow them to exist very long.

If these groups want to maintain their existence, they must act outside the limits of the factory, or they will be destroyed by capital in one way or another. The disappearance of these groups is one of the signs of the radical nature of the movement. If they went on existing as organisations, they would lose their radical character. So they will always disappear and later come to life again in a more radical way. The idea that workers' groups will finally succeed, after many experiments and failures, in forming a powerful organisation capable of overthrowing capitalism, is similar to the bourgeois idea that a partial critique will gradually turn into a radical one. The activity of the working class does not proceed from experiences and has no other "memory" than the general conditions of capital which compel it to act according to its nature. It does not study its experiences; the failure of a movement is itself an adequate demonstration of its limitations.

The communist organisation will grow out of the practical need to transform capitalism into communism. Communist organisation is the organisation of the change from capitalism into communism. Here lies the fundamental difference between our time and the former period. In the struggles which took place between 1917 and 1920 in Russia and Germany, the objective was to organise a pre-communist society. In Russia the radical sections of the working class tried to win over other sections of workers, and even the poor peasants. The isolation of the radical elements and the general conditions of capitalism made it impossible for them to envisage the practical transformation of the entire society without a programme uniting all the exploited classes. These radical elements were eventually crushed.

The difference between our time and the past comes from the vast development of the productive forces on nearly all continents, and the quantitative and qualitative development of the proletariat. The working class is now much more numerous and uses highly developed means of production.[6] Today the conditions of communism have been developed by capital itself. The task of the proletariat is no longer to support progressive sections of capitalists against reactionary ones. The need for a transitional period between the destruction of capitalist power and the triumph of communism, during which the revolutionary power creates the conditions of communism, has also vanished. Therefore there is no place for a communist organisation as a mediation between the radical and non-radical sections of the working class. The fact that an organisation supporting the communist programme fails to emerge during the period between major struggles is the product of a new class relationship in capitalism.

For instance, in France in 1936, the resistance of capital was so strong that a change of government was necessary before the workers could get what they wanted. Today governments themselves initiate the reforms. Capitalist governments try to create situations where the workers organise themselves to achieve what are in fact necessities of production (participation, self-management). Contemporary economy entails more and more planning. Everything outside the plan is a menace to social harmony. Every activity outside this planning is regarded as non-social and must be destroyed. We should keep this in mind when analysing certain activities of workers during periods when there are no mass struggles like strikes or attempted insurrections. The unions must (a) take advantage of workers' struggles and control them, and (b) oppose a number of actions such as sabotage and "downtime" (stopping the line), if they want to stay within the limits of the plan (productivity deals, wage agreements, etc.).

4) Forms of Action Which Cannot Be Recuperated: Sabotage and "Down-timing"

Sabotage has been practised in the United States for many years and is now developing in Italy and France. In 1971, during a railway strike in France, the CGT officially denounced sabotage and "irresponsible" elements. Several engines had been put out of order and a few damaged. Later, in the Renault strike in the Spring of 1971, several acts of sabotage had damaged vehicles which were being assembled. Sabotage is becoming extremely widespread. Stopping the line ("downtiming"), which has always existed as a latent phenomenon, is now becoming a common practice. It has been considerably increased by the arrival of young workers to the labour market, and by automation. It is accompanied by a rate of absenteeism which causes serious trouble to some firms.

These events are not new in the history of capitalism. What is new is the context in which they take place. They are indeed the superficial symptoms of a profound social movement, the signs of a process of breaking away from the existing society. At the beginning of the century, sabotage was used as a means of exerting pressure on the bosses to force them to accept the existence of unions. The French revolutionary unionist Pouget studied this in a pamphlet called *Sabotage*. He quotes the speech of a worker at a workers' congress in 1895: "The bosses have no right to rely on our charity. If they refuse even to discuss our demands, then we can just put into practice the 'Go Canny' tactics, until they decide to listen to us."

Pouget adds: "Here is a clear definition of 'Go Canny' tactics, of 'sabotage': BAD PAY, BAD WORK. This line of action, used by our English friends, can be applied in France, as our social position is similar to that of our English brothers."[7]

Sabotage was used by workers against the boss so that he would admit their existence. It was a way of getting freedom of speech. Sabotage took place in a movement trying to turn the working class into a class which had its place in capitalist society. "Down-timing" was an attempt to improve the conditions of work. Sabotage did not appear as a blunt and direct refusal of society as a whole. "Down-timing" is a fight against the effects of capitalism. Another study will be necessary to examine the limits of such struggles and the conditions in which capital could absorb them. The social importance of these struggles makes it possible to regard them as the basis of "modern reformism." The word "reformism" can be used to the extent that these actions could in theory be completely absorbed by the capitalist system. Whereas today they are a nuisance to the normal activity of production, tomorrow they might well be linked to production. An "ideal" capitalism could tolerate the self-management of the conditions of production: as long as a normal profit is made by the firm, the organisation of the work can be left to the workers.

Capitalism has already carried out some concrete experiments in this direction, particularly in Italy, in the United States, in Sweden (Volvo): the Taylor system as we know it is being transformed, and the assembly line has already partly disappeared in some factories.[8] In France, one may regard left-wing "liberal" organisations such as the PSU, the CFDT and the left of the Socialist Party as the expression of this capitalist tendency.[9] For the time being, this movement can be defined neither as exclusively reformist nor as anti-capitalist. It should be noted that this "'modern reformism" has often been directed against the unions. It is still difficult to describe its consequences on capitalist production. All we can see so far is that these struggles attract groups of workers who feel the need to act outside the traditional boundaries imposed by the unions.

Although the "down-timing movement" can be defined as we have just done, sabotage is different. There are two kinds of sabotage: (a) sabotage which destroys the product of the work or the machine; (b) sabotage which partially damages the product so that it can no longer be consumed. Sabotage as it exists today can in no way be kept in check by the unions, nor can it be absorbed by production. Yet capital can prevent it by improving and transforming its system of supervision. For this reason sabotage cannot become the form of struggle against capital. On the other hand, sabotage is a reflex of the individual: he submits to it, as to a passion. Although the individual must sell his labour power, he goes "mad," i.e. irrational compared to what is "rational" (selling one's labour power and working accordingly). This "madness" consists of the refusal to give up the labour power, to be a commodity. The individual hates himself as an alienated creature split into two; he tries, through destruction, through violence, to re-unify his being, which only exists through capital.

Since these acts are outside the boundaries of all economic planning, they are also outside the boundaries of "reason." Newspapers have repeatedly defined them as "anti-social" and "mad": the danger appears important enough for society to try to suppress it.[10] Christian ideology admitted the suffering and social inequality of the workers; today capitalist ideology imposes equality in the face of wage-labour, but does not tolerate anything opposed to wage-labour. The need felt by the isolated individual to oppose physically his practical transformation into a being totally subjected to capital, shows that this submission is more and more intolerable. Destructive acts are part of an attempt to destroy the mediation of wage labour as the only form of social community. In the silence of the proletariat, sabotage appears as the first stammer of human speech.

Both activities, "down-timing" and sabotage, require a certain amount of agreement among the people working where these activities take place. This shows that, although no formal or official organisation appears, there exists an underground network of relations with an anti-capitalist basis. Such a network is more or less dense according to the importance of the activity, and it disappears with the end of the anti-capitalist action. It is normal that, apart from the "subversive" practical (and therefore theoretical) action, the groups gathered around these subversive tasks should dissolve. Often the need to maintain an illusion of "social community" results in an activity which is secondarily anti-capitalist but primarily illusory. In most cases these groups end up by gathering around some political axis. In France nuclei of workers gather around such organisations as the Trotskyist "Lutte Ouvrière," a number of CFDT union branches, or Maoist groups. This does not mean that some minorities with Trotskyist, Maoist, or CFDT ideas are gaining ground among the workers, but simply that some workers' minorities are trying to break their isolation, which is quite normal. In all cases, the dissolution of the anti-capitalist network and activity means the re-organisation of the working class by capital, as a part of capital.

In short, apart from its practical activities, the communist movement does not exist. The dissolution of a social disorder with a communist content is accompanied by the dissolution of the entire system of relations which it organised. Democracy, division of struggles into "economic" and "political" struggles, formation of a vanguard with a socialist "consciousness," are the illusions of days gone by. These illusions are no longer possible to the extent that a new period is beginning. The dissolution of the organisational forms which are created by the movement, and which disappear when the movement ends, does not reflect the weakness of the movement, but rather its strength. The time of false battles is over. The only conflict that appears real is the one that leads to the destruction of capitalism.

5) Parties and Unions in the Face of the Communist Perspective

5.1

On the labour market, unions increasingly become monopolies which help buy and sell labour power. When it unified itself, capital unified the conditions of the sale of labour power. In modern conditions of production, the individual owner of labour power is not only forced to sell it to be able to live, but must also associate with other owners in order to be able to sell it. In return for social peace, the unions got the right to control the hiring of labour. In modern society workers are increasingly compelled to join the union if they want to sell their labour power.

At the beginning of this century, unions were the product of gatherings of workers who formed coalitions to defend the average selling price of their commodity. The unions were not at all revolutionary, as was shown by their attitude in World War I, when they supported the war both directly and indirectly. In so far as the workers were fighting for their existence as a class within capitalist society, the unions had no revolutionary function. In Germany, during the revolutionary upheaval of 1919–1920, the union members went to organisations which defended their economic rights in the general context of the struggle against capitalism, such as the Shop Stewards' Movement in Britain, the French Revolutionary Syndicalist Committees, and the German General Workers' Association (AAUD). Outside of a revolutionary period, the working class is nothing but a fraction of capital represented by the unions. While other fractions of capital (industrial and financial capital) are forming monopolies, the working class as variable capital also form a monopoly, of which the unions are the trustees.

5.2

The unions developed at the end of the nineteenth and the beginning of the twentieth century as organisations defending skilled labour power. This was particularly clear with the rise of the AFL in the United States. Until World War II (or until the birth of the CIO in the 1930s in the U.S.) unions grew by supporting the relatively privileged sections of the working class. This is not to say that they had no influence on the most exploited strata, but this influence was only possible if it was consistent with the interests of the qualified strata. With the development of modern and automated industry, highly skilled workers tend to be replaced by technicians. These technicians also have the function of controlling and supervising masses of unskilled workers. Therefore the unions, while losing important sections of workers whose qualifications fade away, try to recruit this new stratum of technicians.

5.3

The unions represent labour power which has become capital. This forces them to appear as institutions capable of valorising capital. The unions have to associate their own development programme with that of industrial and finance capital if they want to keep "'their" labour power under control. The representatives of variable capital, of capital in the form of labour power, sooner or later have to associate with the representatives of fractions of capital who are now in power. Government coalitions consisting of liberal bourgeoisie, technocrats, left-wing political groups, and unions, appear as a necessity in the evolution of capitalism. Capital itself requires strong unions capable of proposing economic measures which can valorise variable capital. The unions are not "traitors" in the sense that they betray the programme of the working class: they are quite consistent with themselves, and with the working class when it accepts its capitalist nature.

5.4

This is how we can understand the relationship between the working class and the unions. When the process of breaking away from capitalist society begins, the unions are immediately seen through and treated in terms of what they are; but as soon as the process ends, the working class cannot help being re-organised by capital, namely by the unions. One may say that there are no "unionist" illusions in the working class. There is only a capitalist, namely "unionist," organisation of the working class.

5.5

The development of the current relationships between unions and bosses in Italy illustrates what has been said. The evolution of Italian unions should be closely watched. It is normal that in relatively backward areas (from an economic point of view) such as France and Italy (compared to the United States), the effects of the modernisation of the economy are accompanied by the most modern tendencies of capital. What happens in Italy is in many ways a sign of what is maturing in other countries.

The Italian situation helps us understand the French one. In France the CGT and the PCF put up a reactionary resistance in the face of workers' struggles, whereas in Italy the CGIL and the PCI have been able to re-shape themselves in terms of the new situation. This is one of the reasons for the difference between the French "May" and the Italian "May." In France, May 1968 happened suddenly and could be easily misunderstood. The Italian situation proceeds more slowly and ultimately reveals its tendencies.

The first phase lasted from 1968 to the winter of 1971. The main element was the birth of workers' struggles independent of the influence of unions and political organisations. Workers' action committees were formed as in France, with one essential difference: the French ones were quickly driven out of the factories by the power of the unions, which in practice compelled them to have no illusions about the boundaries of the factory. Insofar as the general situation did not allow them to go any further, they disappeared. In Italy, on the other hand, workers' committees were at first able to organise themselves inside the factories. Neither the bosses nor the unions could really oppose them. Many committees were formed in the factories, in isolation from each other, and they all began to question the speed of the assembly line and to organise sabotage.

This was in fact an alienated form of critique of wage-labour. Throughout the Italian movement the activity of far-left groups (*gauchistes*) was particularly noteworthy. Their entire activity consisted of limiting the movement to its formal aspects without ever showing its real content. They bred the illusion that the "autonomy" of workers' organisations was in itself revolutionary enough to be supported and maintained. They glorified all the formal aspects. But since they are not communists, they were not able to express the idea that behind the struggle against the rhythm of the line and the working conditions lay the struggle against wage-labour.

The workers' struggle itself met no resistance. This was in fact what disarmed it. It could do nothing but adapt to the conditions of capitalist society. The unions, for their part, altered their structures in order to control the workers' movement. As Trentin, one of the leaders of the CGIL, said, they decided to organise "a thoroughgoing transformation of the union and a new type of rank-and-file democracy." They re-shaped their factory organisations according to the pattern of the "autonomous" committees which appeared in recent struggles. The ability of the unions to control industrial strife made them appear as the only force capable of making the workers resume work. There were negotiations in some large concerns like Fiat. The result of these negotiations was to give the union the right to interfere in the organisation of work (time and motion, work measurement, etc.). The management of Fiat now deducts the union dues from the workers' pay, which was already the case in Belgium. At the same time, serious efforts are being made to reach an agreement on a merger between the biggest unions: the Socialist UIL, the Christian-Democrat CISL, and the Italian CP-led GGIL.[11]

The Italian example clearly shows the tendency of unions to become monopolies which discuss the conditions of production of surplus-value with other fractions of capital. Here are quotations from Petrilli, president of the State-owned IRI (State Holding Company), and Trentin:

Trentin: "Job enrichment and the admission of a higher degree of autonomy in decision-making by the workers' group concerned (in each factory) are already possible. . . . Even when, because of the failure of the union, workers' protests lead to irrational and illusory demands, the workers express their refusal to produce without thinking, to work without deciding; they express their need for power."

Petrilli: "In my opinion it is obvious that the system of the assembly line implies a real waste of human capacities and produces a very understandable feeling of frustration in the worker. The resulting social tensions must be realistically understood as structural rather than conjunctural facts. . . . Greater participation of the workers in the elaboration of production objectives poses a series of problems having to do less with the organisation of work than with the definition of the power balance within the firm."

The programmes are identical and the aims are the same: increased productivity. The only remaining problem is the sharing of power, which is at the root of the political crisis in many industrial countries. It is likely that the end of the political crisis will be accompanied by the birth of "workers' power" as the power of wage-labour, under various forms: self-management, "popular" coalitions, Socialist-Communist Parties, left-wing governments with right-wing programmes, right-wing governments with left-wing programmes.[12]

CHAPTER 3

■ A CRASH COURSE IN ULTRA-LEFTOLOGY

1) Out of the Past

Palmiro Togliatti, long-time Stalinist and long-time leader of the Italian CP, once called Amadeo Bordiga an iguanodon. Though dinosaurs roamed the Earth for much longer than the human species probably will, one may ask: Why bother about the Communist left?

A good enough reason is that it was the most acute expression of the proletarian movement in the twentieth century, even if the historical situation prevented it from implementing its options and solutions: only at the end of the 1960s were left Communist deeds and ideas revived when a period emerged that needed to re-appropriate the past and pick up historical threads.

2) Beyond Words and Beyond Belief

Ultra-left is nearly always a derogatory term. In the early 1920s, the Communist International called "ultra-leftists" those communists who were anti-union and anti-parliament, mainly the German-Dutch opposition (the KAPD), less so the "abstentionist" Italian CP led by Bordiga. Lenin's *Left-Wing Communism: An Infantile Disorder* (1920) advocated "utmost flexibility" as a remedy against ultra-leftist "rigid doctrinairism."

The word was later applied to the Third International for its *class against class* "sectarian" period (1929–34), before the Popular Front policy. In the 1930s, Trotsky called some of his critics "ultra-left phrase mongers," and used the term in his polemic on the Spanish question against the Belgian-Italian group which published *Bilan*. It was also a Stalinist label applied to Trotskyists. Today it has become a media blanket term for violent radicals. The word is a condensed story in its own right, which begets as much confusion as *communism* or *anarchism*.

"Leninism and the Ultra-Left" will deal mostly with "German-Dutch" councilism, but we will have to say a few words on the "Italian" left.

The German-Dutch left and the Italian left had a lot more in common than is usually thought . . . and than either of them believed. Anton Pannekoek regarded Amadeo Bordiga as a weird sectarian pro-Lenin Marxist, and Bordiga viewed Pannekoek as a misconceived mixture of Marxism and anarcho-syndicalism. Neither took any real interest in the other, and like strangers who share the same story the "German" and "Italian" communist lefts largely ignored each other. Both did for a reason, and our purpose is not to reconcile them: each to his own mistakes.

Since the first draft of "Leninism and the Ultra-Left" (1969), a wealth of information has been made public, first in print and now a lot more online.[1] Yet the world web is like an endless book that provides an infinity of answers (with thousands more added every hour); only the questions are missing. The Net-surfer is a traveller equipped with a map the size of the country he wishes to explore. What we lack is not data: it is the angle, the approach.

3) The German-Dutch Left

To this day, the 1917–37 years remain a historical watershed. At the end of the 1914–18 war, millions felt they were taking part in the birth of a new era, "when Communism like the morning dawns," in the words of Sylvia Pankhurst (*Writ on*

Cold Slate, 1920–21: she led the first CP created in Britain in 1919). Anton Pannekoek (1873–1960), Herman Gorter (1864–1927), Otto Rühle (1874–1943) and later Paul Mattick (1904–1981) had expressed (and contributed to organise) some of the most profound features of this post-1917 epoch-making movement.

Though they were mostly active in Germany, some major contributors were Dutch-born, hence the word "German-Dutch." Socialists in the Netherlands were among the very few before 1914 who kept alive a revolutionary spirit: when the left split in 1909 to form its own party, it was the first split of that kind in Western Europe (only the Russians and Bulgarians had done so).

During the war, what later became the German left took a firm anti-patriotic stand, as the Russian and Serbian socialist parties did, as well as small minorities like the Irish Trades Union Congress led by J. Connolly, the Jewish Bund, or the "Narrow" Bulgarian socialists.

At the end of 1918, at its founding congress, the German CP (KPD) refused to take part in the forthcoming elections, against the opinion of Rosa Luxemburg who thought possible some revolutionary parliamentary action. A few months later, the left found itself a minority in the KPD and split to create the KAPD: the "A" (*Arbeiter*) emphasised that the new party claimed to be the authentic expression of working class interest, against bourgeois and bureaucrats alike. Meanwhile in the Netherlands, the "left" socialist party gave birth to a communist party in 1918, only to split in 1920, which resulted in a Communist Workers' Party similar to but much smaller than its German equivalent.

Political events reflected a momentous social change. In the German rampant civil war from 1919 to 1923, the most active workers had created new forms of organisation, *Unionen*, which did not mean trade-unions (*Gewerkschaften* in German): the *Unionen* actually fought the trade-unions. A major difference between the *Unionen* and previous forms was the will to go beyond the union/party or economy/politics differentiation.

For a couple of years, the *Unionen* gathered several hundred thousand workers.

This evolution was made explicit in Pannekoek's essay "World Revolution and Communist Tactics" (1920), one of the most far-sighted writings of that period. Pannekoek saw that the failure of the Second International was not due to the failure of its strategy, but that the strategy was rooted in the function and form of the Second International: the parties and unions that collapsed in 1914 had been adapted to a precise stage of capitalism, in which workers fought for economic and political reforms . . . and were granted some. To make the revolution, the proletariat had to build organs of a new type, which would go beyond the old party/union dichotomy. A conflict with the Bolshevik-led Comintern was unavoidable. First, because the Russians had never fully understood what the old International had been, and believed in organising the workers from above, without seeing the connection between Kautsky's "socialist consciousness" introduced into the masses, and Kautsky's passive radicalism. Secondly, because the Russian State needed mass worker parties in Europe, capable of putting pressure on their governments to come to terms with Russia as a reborn power.

The social waves ebbed and flowed, soon the real proletarian element faced an uphill battle, and various large non-communist Communist Parties developed in the West. Many workers believed Leninism was providing them with a fire-tested doctrine, when it was actually consolidating a new variant of reformism. After 1921, KAPD membership quickly declined. The same happened in Bulgaria. Sylvia Pankhurst gradually drifted away from communism. The *Worker* Communist International launched in 1923 was still-born. Nothing could revitalise a proletariat caught between social-democracy and Leninism (soon Stalinism). The die was cast. The aftershocks of the early 1920s rumbled on, the '29 crash radicalised social strife with little revolutionary content, the communist left was reduced to small groups divided into different factions, and only a few hundred members were still active in Germany when Hitler took power.

The German left's perception of union and party bureaucracies as forms that channelled and chained worker self-awareness and activity went parallel to its analysis of post-1917 Russia as a society led by a new exploitative class. As early as 1920, after a stay in Russia, Otto Rühle wrote that the workers were as much oppressed there as in Germany. In Western countries, union and party leaders acted as the representatives of the workers within capitalism: in the so-called "land of the soviets," the Bolshevik leadership was fulfilling the task that the traditional bourgeoisie had proved incapable of achieving. In *Lenin as Philosopher* (1938), Pannekoek went further: not only had the Russian revolution been made by the workers for the benefit of a bureaucratic ruling class, but basic Bolshevik tenets owed more to bourgeois philosophy and outlook than to proletarian Marxism.

Of special interest to us is how the German-Dutch left envisaged communism. In the early 1930s, the Dutch group GIK (with further developments by Paul Mattick) set forth what has become the classic "councilist" view, in *The Fundamental Principles of Communist Production and Distribution*. Whereas capitalism is production for value accumulation, communism is production for use value, for the fulfilment of people's needs. Contrary to bourgeois anarchy and bureaucratic planning, so the argument goes, worker councils will organise an accurate system of *labour time* bookkeeping, without the mediation of money, in order to keep track of the amount of labour time contained in every produced item.

In *Workers' Councils*, started during the war and completed in 1947, Pannekoek epitomised the councilist vision where worker councils became the means and the end of revolution and of the future society:

> How will the quantities of labour spent and the quantities
> of product to which [every worker] is entitled be meas-
> ured? In a society where the goods are produced directly

for consumption there is no market to exchange them; and no value, as expression of the labour contained in them establishes itself automatically out of the processes of buying and selling. Here the labour spent must be expressed in a direct way by the number of hours. The administration keeps records of the hours of labour contained in every piece or unit quantity of product, as well as of the hours spent by each of the workers. In the averages over all the workers of a factory, and finally, over all the factories of the same category, the personal differences are smoothed out and the personal results are inter-compared. (Part 1, section 4)

This crucial issue will be dealt with at more length in chapter 5 in connection with Marx. For the moment, suffice it to say that it was an immense breakthrough to try and define communism and, above all, to do it by investigating value which hardly anybody else bothered about at the time. And that pursuit would have been impossible without the *practical* breakthrough that the proletarians strove to achieve in the 1920s and '30s. As our chapter 5 will argue, the snag is that, value being the amount of social labour-time necessary to produce an item, a rational accounting system in labour-time would be equivalent to the rule of value without the medium of money.

Worker self-activity is vital to proletarian emancipation: that is the indispensable legacy of council communism. But when that essential notion fostered the thesis that communism is self-managed work, council communism reached a point which turned it into ideology: councilism.

Besides, for a considerable number of council communists, the (justified) opposition to union and party grew into a principle above all else, and was interpreted as a rejection of any action that risked impose itself on the working class. Revolutionaries, the belief runs, only have to correspond, set forth theory, circulate information, and describe what the workers are doing. Everything has to come from the class. Communists must not organise to define a strategy, or act accordingly, lest they become the new leaders of the workers and later the new ruling class.

4) Bordiga

To make the most of the German-Dutch left, a few words on the "other" Communist left, the Italian left, can be of assistance. Whereas Pannekoek came to a complete rejection of Bolshevism and from the 1930s interpreted the Russian revolution as an anti-bourgeoisie capitalist revolution, Amadeo Bordiga (1889–1970) always maintained he only had *tactical* disagreements with Lenin, and even wrote in 1960 in defence of *An Infantile Disorder*. So nothing looks further apart than "Bordigism" and "council communism."

The situation goes a lot deeper than that.

Like Pannekoek, who had fought against reformism before the war and even split the Dutch Socialist Party to create a new one, Bordiga belonged to the left of his party. But Italian radicals did not venture as far as the Dutch ones. At the time of the First World War, Italian socialism kept a somewhat radical outlook, so there was little opportunity for or desire of a split. The party even opposed Italy's joining in the conflict in 1915, albeit in a passive way.

At the end of the war, the Abstentionist faction led by Bordiga prevailed among the radicals who founded the Italian CP in 1921. Contrary to what was happening in France and Germany at the same time, the new party was born out of a break not just with the right of the old party, but also with its centre. This was the exact opposite of what the Comintern wanted. In any case, the proletarians found themselves in an intractable challenge, locked between a parliamentary regime they could not overthrow and a rising fascist movement, and the party was unable to reverse the downhill trend. After Mussolini took power, the party leadership went to Gramsci in 1923, forcing Bordiga into minority and opposition, until he was expelled from the Italian CP in 1930.

The Italian left's attitude on the parliamentary question, the *united front* tactics, the *workers' government* policy and, last but not least, on anti-fascism, is well documented enough for us not to deal with those issues here. The books and sites mentioned in our note are also very informative on what the so-called Bordigists did in the 1930s and later, especially in Italy, Belgium, and France. Let us just say that, at least until 1926, and unlike the German left, Bordiga refused to explain the Bolsheviks' and the International's positions in terms of the degeneration of the Russian State and party. He felt the Comintern was wrong, but was still communist. At the Executive Committee of the Communist International in 1926 and in Stalin's presence, Bordiga harshly criticised the Russian leaders: this was probably the last time a revolutionary openly attacked them from within at such a high level, and lived to tell the tale. Yet at that time Bordiga still failed to define Russia as capitalist.

In a nutshell, Bordiga supported Lenin but was no Leninist: his conception of the party was different in theory and practice. He did not think "socialist (or communist) consciousness" had to be introduced into the working class from an outside group of revolutionaries who would then organise a party based on workers' cells centralised around a theory-providing leadership. Unlike some of his comrades within the Italian left, in particular after 1945, Bordiga was no party-builder at all costs. He never subscribed to Trotsky's theory that "The historical crisis of mankind is reduced to the crisis of the revolutionary leadership" (Fourth International's *Transitional Programme*, 1938).

However, his belief that Lenin's options for Western communists were tactical mistakes, and above all his inability to see the reality of what had happened to the Russian workers and peasants soon after 1917, show how he conceived the proletariat. He never understood that the Russian revolution had failed as early as 1919–21, because he thought it possible for a fully-committed communist minority to seize power, keep it for years, and serve as a support point that would hold the fort until revolution erupted elsewhere. To put it bluntly, revolution from above: though Bordiga never ignored proletarian self-activity, he did not regard it as a necessary condition of communist revolution.

5) The Salient Point

Now the polemical dust has settled, and our purpose is not to deal out blame or merit.

Both Pannekoek and Bordiga had a much broader perspective and world-view than most. Though Bordiga kept disclaiming adding any novelty to pure and simple theory of the proletariat, he was an innovative thinker, particularly after 1945, on ecology, Marx's early works, community, ancient society . . . Pannekoek showed similar, if lesser, interest, for instance in his *Anthropogenesis* (1944). Both thought there was a lot more in capitalism and class struggle than capitalism and class struggle. In spite of councilism and party-ism, or via a councilist bias and a party bias, they broached communism and proletariat in all their dimensions.

Today, and only today, as the next two chapters will argue, we can understand why the attempt to define communism made by the GIK, Mattick, and Pannekoek later was basically flawed. And our re-examination of Marx will help get a clearer picture of the German-Dutch left.

All in all, it will prove a lot more than a trip down failed revolution memory lane.

(G.D., 2013)

CHAPTER 4

■ LENINISM AND THE ULTRA-LEFT

As explained in the previous chapter, we will deal here mostly with *council communism*, or what is known as the German-Dutch left. Its invaluable merit was and remains to hammer in the primacy of workers' self-activity and spontaneity: the potentialities of communism lie in proletarian experience and nowhere else. This "ultra-left" has therefore consistently appealed to the essence of the proletariat against its numerous mistaken forms of existence. From the 1920s, it has stood against all mediations, whether State, party, or union, including breakaway unions, splinter groups and even anarchist unions such as the CNT. If Lenin can be summed up in one word: "party," a single phrase defines the ultra-left: *the workers themselves* . . . nothing wrong with that. The question is: which workers' "self" is meant?

This issue must be faced, all the more so since council communism, through the Situationist International, has become quite influential. Guy Debord was a member of the French group Socialisme ou Barbarie in 1960–61, a lot of "social-barbarism" was incorporated in the SI, and the call for workers' councils became one of the prime Situationist themes.[1]

The first French draft of this text (1969) originated from a group with ultra-left roots. The essay's main writer had authored an analysis of the Russian revolution published a couple of months before May '68: the text made the point that in 1917–21 the Russian working class had strived to achieve worker control or even worker management, only to be defeated by the Bolshevik party which finally replaced the bourgeoisie as the new ruling class. The text equated communism with worker management.[2] The experience of the '68 general strike (as reflected in François Martin's analysis, for example), plus a growing interest in the Italian left, convinced several members of this informal group that council communism required serious re-examination, the upshot of which was the first draft of this text, written for a convention organised by ICO (Informations & Correspondances Ouvrières), held near Paris, June 1969.[3] In fact, our essay targeted more ICO's version of councilism than councilism in general. We knew of the Situationists' critique of ICO. While the *SI*'s eleventh issue wrote "we strongly recommend reading [ICO] for an understanding of the current workers' struggles," it added the rider:

> There is, however, one fundamental opposition: we believe in the necessity of formulating a precise theoretical critique of the present society of exploitation. We consider that such a theoretical formulation can only be produced by an organised collectivity; and inversely we think that any present permanent liaison organised with workers must attempt to discover a general theoretical basis for its action. What *On the Poverty of Student Life* described as ICO's choice of non-existence in this domain does not mean that we think that the ICO comrades lack ideas or theoretical knowledge, but on the contrary that by intentionally putting these diverse ideas in parenthesis, they lose more than they gain in their capacity for unification (which is, in the end, of the highest practical importance).[4]

By and large, we agreed with this critique, and still do.

Over the years, "Leninism and the Ultra-Left" has been called "prototypal" or "seminal" (usually more a dismissal than a compliment), and gone through several titles, versions, and editions: 1969, 1972, 1973, 1997, now 2013. Former editions had sections on labour and value inspired by Marx's views, which we are now convinced need re-appraisal. For clarity purposes, and to avoid repetitions, we have chosen to delete those passages, and only to engage in a critique of Marx in the following chapter.

(1997–2013)

The ultra-left was far from monolithic. As we will see, Herman Gorter's *Open Letter to Lenin* (1920) formulates a theory of the party which differs from Lenin's, but still leaves room for a party, a conception most council communists—Pannekoek among others—no longer accept. On the two decisive points ("organisation" and the content of communism), we shall only consider the ideas which the ultra-left has retained throughout its development. The French group ICO is one of the best examples of a present-day ultra-left group.

1) Party or Council?

Ultra-left ideas are the product of a practical experience (mainly the workers' struggles in Germany) and of a theoretical critique (the critique of Leninism). For Lenin, the supreme revolutionary problem was to forge a "leadership" capable of leading the workers to victory. On the basis of the rise of mass factory organisations in Germany, the German left said the working class needed no leaders. Revolution would be made by self-organised workers' councils and not under the guidance of professional revolutionaries. The German Communist Workers' Party (KAPD), whose aim and tactic were probably best expressed by Gorter, regarded itself as a vanguard whose task was to enlighten the masses, not to conduct them as in Leninist theory.

This conception was rejected by many ultra-leftists, who opposed the *dual* existence of the factory organisations and the party: revolutionaries must not try to organise themselves in a body distinct from the masses. Part of the KAPD—Otto Rühle in particular—called for the immediate abolition of the party organisation, and logically left the KAPD. In the AAUD (General Union of German Workers), which gathered together many *Unionen*, a tendency developed against what it regarded as harmful leadership by the KAPD, and created a new gathering, the AAUD-E, the "E" (*Einheitsorganisation*) standing for *unitary* organisation, viz. beyond the economic/political division. The AAUD-E reproached the AAUD with being controlled by the KAPD in the same way as the official

CP controlled the trade-unions. Most council communists later adopted the same view as the AAUD-E. In France, ICO's present activity is based on the same principle: any revolutionary organisation coexisting with the organs created by the workers themselves, and trying to elaborate a coherent theory and political line, must in the end attempt to take control over the workers. Therefore revolutionaries do not organise themselves outside the organs "spontaneously" created by the workers: they merely exchange and circulate information, and establish contacts with other revolutionaries; they never try to define a general theory or strategy.

This is the exact opposite of Leninism. Lenin's theory of the party is based on a distinction common to quite a few socialist thinkers of the period: "labour movement" and "socialism" (revolutionary ideas, Scientific Socialism, Marxism, etc.—it goes by many names) are two different realities. Compare Kautsky's *The Three Sources of Marxism* (1907) and Lenin's *Three Sources and Three Components of Marxism* (1913): both interpret the making of modern proletarian revolutionary thought as the fusion of German philosophy, English political economy and French socialism and utopianism, i.e. an intellectual construct, elaborated by bourgeois-born intellectuals.[5] Labour movement and revolutionary movement must be united through the leadership of the latter over the former. Therefore revolutionaries must get organised and act on the working class "from the outside." Unless socialists "introduce" socialism into the working class, that class can only fight bread-and-butter issues.

Kautsky-Lenin's starting point seems based on facts: a university-educated person is more familiar with reading and writing than a plumber who left school in his teens. Yet who holds the pen is inessential. Marx's writings were an expression of the struggle of the proletariat. Even if communist thought was articulated by "bourgeois intellectuals" (and by highly educated workers like Joseph Dietzgen, a self-taught tanner who developed his own materialist conception of history), it was spawned by class confrontation. In the twentieth century, theoreticians as important as Paul Mattick and Jan Appel were both manual workers.

Instead of explaining "class consciousness" by class experience, Kautsky and Lenin derived experience from consciousness. Lenin knew perfectly well that revolution was made by spontaneous mass action (in that sense, he was no bureaucrat), but thought it could only succeed with proper leadership built from outside.

This was in stark contrast to Marx's conception of the party. There is no text which sums up his ideas on the subject, only scattered remarks, yet a general view emerges: capitalist society generates a communist party, not in the primarily political sense, but as the organisation of the objective movement that is at work within society and can lead to communist revolution. This movement is objective because it is not created by consciousness, though of course it is expressed consciously in various conflicting ways.

> After the "League" had been disbanded at my behest in November 1852, I never belonged to any society again, whether secret or public; . . . the party, therefore, in this wholly ephemeral sense, ceased to exist for me eight years ago . . . since 1852 I had not been associated with any association and was firmly convinced that my theoretical studies were of greater use to the working class than my meddling with associations which had now had their day on the Continent. Because of this "inactivity" I was thereupon repeatedly and bitterly attacked. . . . Since 1852, then, I have known nothing of "party" in the sense implied in your letter. . . . The "League", like the Société des Saisons in Paris and a hundred other societies, was simply an episode in the history of a party that is everywhere springing up naturally out of the soil of modern society. . . . I have tried to dispel the misunderstanding arising out of the impression that by "party" I meant a "League" that expired eight years ago, or an editorial board that was disbanded twelve years ago. By party, I meant the party in the broad historical sense.[6]

This "party" is neither created nor not-to-be-created: it is a product and an expression of the proletariat (often identified with the working class in Marx's writings), and less an organisation than a programme, a perspective, held by at least an active minority. This is miles away from Kautsky's and Lenin's conception of a "socialist consciousness" which must be "brought" to the workers.

Lenin misunderstood class struggle. In a non-revolutionary period the proletariat cannot change capitalist production relations. It therefore tries to change capitalist distribution relations through its demand for higher wages. Of course the workers do not "know" that they are changing the distribution relations when they ask for higher wages. Yet they do try, "unconsciously," to act upon the capitalist system. Kautsky's and Lenin's theory of class consciousness breaks up a process and considers one of its transitory moments: for them the proletariat "by its own resources alone" can only be reformist. In this education-centred view of history, the workers are promising children who yet have to go to school. In actual fact, revolutionaries as well as their ideas are born in workers' struggles.

In a non-revolutionary period, revolutionary workers, isolated in their factories, do their best to expose the real nature of capitalism and the institutions which support it (State, unions, "worker" parties). They usually do this with little success, which is quite normal. And there are revolutionaries (workers and non-workers) who read and write, who do their best to provide a critique of the whole system. They usually do this with little success, which is also quite normal. This division is a result of capitalism: a characteristic of capitalist society is the division between manual and intellectual work. This division exists in all social spheres, therefore also in the revolutionary movement, which is a product of our society and bears the stigma of capitalism.

Only the complete success of revolution will do away with this division: until then, we must challenge this separation, but we cannot help it having effects on our movement as much as it affects society as a whole. It is inevitable that numerous revolutionaries are not greatly inclined to reading, and show little interest in theory. This is a fact, a transitory fact. But "revolutionary workers" and "revolutionary theoreticians" are two aspects of the same process. It is wrong to say that the "theoreticians" must lead the "workers." When ICO maintains that collectively organised theory could result in leadership over the workers, it takes a position opposed to but *symmetrically* opposed to Lenin's. The revolutionary process is an organic process, and although its components may act separately for a certain time, the advent of any historical tremor starts getting them together.

What happened in May 1968 in the worker-student action committees at the Censier centre in Paris? Some (ultra-left) communists, who before these events had devoted most of their revolutionary activity to theory, met up with a minority of radical workers. Before May 1968 (and since then), they were no more separate from the workers than every worker is separate from his fellow workers in a non-revolutionary situation. Marx was no more estranged from the working class when he was writing *Das Kapital* than when he was active in the Communist League or the First International. In these organisations, he felt neither the urge (as Lenin), nor the fear (as ICO), to become the leader of the workers.

Marx's conception of the party as a historical product taking different forms according to the evolution of society enables us to go beyond the dilemma: need of the party/ allergy to the party. The communist party is the spontaneous (i.e. totally determined by social evolution) organisation of the revolutionary movement created by capitalism. The party is a spontaneous offspring of the soil of modern society. There is no point in attempting to "build the party," nor in refraining from it.

Marx had a theory of the party. Lenin had another, which contributed to the Bolsheviks' seizure of power, and then played its part in the defeat of the revolution, as it cemented together a ruling elite which thought of itself as separate from and superior to the toiling masses. This encouraged the ultra-left to reject all theories of the party. Yet Lenin's theory was not *the cause* of the revolutionary failure in Russia: his conception prevailed because the Russian revolution failed, mainly because of the absence of revolution in the West, and there was a power vacuum in Russia that only the Bolsheviks were there to fill. Why discard all theories of the party because one of them (Lenin's) was a counter-revolutionary instrument? Councilism gave a different answer to the same warped question: *for* or *against* party-building. The ultra-left remained on the same ground as Lenin. Lenin's view is not to be reversed, but abandoned.

Modern Leninists set themselves the Sisyphus goal of organising the masses. Contemporary ultra-left groups (ICO, in particular) only circulate information and avoid adopting a collective position on all the issues we are confronted with. As opposed to this, we believe it necessary to formulate what the SI called a *unitary critique of the world*, which implies collective activity with an attempt at coherence. Any permanent group of revolutionary workers logically looks for a theoretical basis for its action. Theoretical clarification is an element of, and a necessary condition for, practical unification . . .

. . . bearing in mind that in each period, communist theory expresses two things: the highest level reached by the previous insurrectionary phase; and the elements in contemporary proletarian struggles which seem to herald the content of new insurrections to come. Therefore radical theory can never avoid expressing its overall "historical" perspective within the inevitable limits of its time. The *incompleteness* of communist theory reflects the in-between-two-worlds situation of the proletarians.

2) Managing What?
The Russian revolution died when it ended up developing capitalism in Russia. To create an efficient body of managers became its watchword. The German-Dutch left concluded that bureaucratic management could not bring

about socialism—which was true, and which many people (Trotskyists for instance) failed to understand—and it advocated workers' management, which is inadequate. A self-contained conception was born, with workers' councils at its centre: the councils act as the fighting organs of the workers under capitalism and as the instruments of workers' management under socialism. Thus the councils play the same pivotal role in ultra-left theory as the party in Leninism.

The theory of workers' management analyses capitalism in terms of who runs it. But is capitalism first of all a mode of management? The analysis of capitalism initiated by Marx does not lay the stress on who manages it: Marx described both capitalists and workers as functions in a productive system: "the capitalist as such is only a function of capital, the labourer a function of labour power." The Russian bureaucratic leaders do not "lead" the economy; they are led by it, and the development of the Russian economy obeys the objective laws of capitalist accumulation. A manager is no autocrat. Capitalism is not a mode of *management* but a mode of *production* based on specific *productive relations*, and revolution targets these relations. Russian and American managers only wield power in as much as they pander to the requirements of value and productivity.

Of course production relations are personified in the concrete existence of worker v. boss, but the leader/led opposition is a form of the fundamental capital/wage-labour relation. The function of capitalist tends to be separate from the function of worker: "order-takers" will never be "order-givers," to use a vocabulary favoured by Castoriadis and the late Socialisme ou Barbarie.

Let us confront Lenin with Marx:

> The fundamental problem of any revolution is the problem of power. (Lenin)

> In all revolutions up till now the mode of activity always remained unscathed and it was only a question of a different distribution of this activity, a new distribution of

labour to other persons, whilst the communist revolution is directed against the preceding, does away with labour ... and abolishes the rule of all classes with the classes themselves, because it is carried through by the class which no longer counts as a class in society, is not recognised as a class, and is in itself the expression of the dissolution of all classes, nationalities, etc. within present society. (Marx)[7]

In a bourgeois revolution, the fundamental problem may well be power. In a communist revolution, power certainly matters ... in so far as it helps create a "mode of activity" that "does away with labour," and this creation is fundamental.

The Bolshevik bureaucracy took the economy under its control. Council communists want democratically-organised workers to do this. It remains on the same ground as Leninism: it once again gives a different answer to a similar question: how to run the economy. Let's replace that question with a different one: the destruction of that economy, which is capitalist.[8]

3) The Historical Limit of the Ultra-Left

Communist revolution is the process by which the proletariat terminates the historical course of capital. The proletariat does more than seize the world: it puts an end to the objective dynamics which created value, commodity, and wage-labour, and spread them all over the planet. Marx insisted on substance, Lenin and the ultra-left on forms: form of political organisation, form of social management. This, too, was a historical product: the situation of the period prevented revolutionary struggles from having a communist content.

When they kept repeating that the masses needed leaders, the Bolsheviks expressed the impossibility of revolution in their time. Councilism expressed its necessity, without situating exactly where its possibility lay. This was an era of large reformist organisations, social-democrat and Stalinist ones: it took little time for "communist" parties to sink into another variant of reformism. The post-1917 revolutionary wave did not go deep enough for a communist perspective to emerge, so everywhere, in Germany, in Italy, in France, in Britain, in the United States, the working class soon fell back under the control of "worker" leaders. Reacting against this situation, at the same time as they affirmed an indispensable and *still valid* critique of unionism, parliamentarianism, "worker" parties and vanguardism, council communists were driven to the point where they feared to become the new bureaucrats. Instead of understanding Leninist parties as a product of proletarian defeat, they theorised diametrically opposed organisational forms and, like Lenin, ignored the Marxian conception of the party. As for the content of communism, no social movements, except in Spain for a short time after 1936, really endeavoured to overthrow capitalism.[9] In such conditions, it was unlikely for any segment of the Communist left to come close to a profound critique of Leninism. Misinterpreting the content of revolution was all the more inevitable as actual struggles hardly manifested that content.

Revolution *has*, but *is not* a problem of organisation. The main point is not that unions or political parties are inadequate vehicles for proletarian emancipation. Indeed they are. Communist revolution being an altogether different phenomenon from bourgeois revolution and implying a break with bourgeois society, it requires completely different modes of organisation: O. Rühle was perfectly right to explain in 1920 that "The Revolution Is Not a Party Affair." Yet the heart of the matter is that autonomous proletarian bodies only retain their autonomy if they engage in tasks which tear away the social fabric, if self-organised collectives initiate value-less and work-less means and ways of life, which force them to confront the State, etc, and it is this process we have to shed light on.

Councilism replaced the Leninist fetishism of the party and class-consciousness with the fetishism of workers' councils. The critique of both Leninism and ultra-leftism is now possible because the development of capitalism, and the struggles that question it, give us a better understanding of what communist revolution means.

Holding on to such basic ultra-left notions as fear of party-building and workers' management would turn them into mere ideology. When these ideas first appeared around 1920, they were not "mistakes," they were the highest possible level of consciousness of hundreds of thousands of strikers and insurgents embarked on a dramatic combat with the bourgeois State, social democracy and Leninism. But things have changed a great deal since 1920. Turning limits into theory is a regression. A new revolutionary workers' minority is in a slow process of formation, as was revealed by the 1968 events in France, and by other struggles in several countries.

There exist billions of proletarians. There also exist what could best be called revolutionary groups. In socially quiet times, little interaction occurs between the two. In socially troubled times, revolutionaries are part of proletarian struggles. Prolier-than-thou behaviour and (as a symmetrical complement) guilt at not-being-working-class inevitably appear: if these attitudes develop, they are an unmistakable sign of weakness. A truly deep revolutionary movement tends towards social unification and theoretical coherence.

Until such times come, revolutionaries never hesitate to act collectively to propagate their critique of the existing society. Communists represent and defend the general interests of the movement. Whenever and however they can, they express the whole meaning of what is going on and make practical proposals. If the expression is right and the proposal appropriate, they become part of proletarian struggle and contribute to build the informal, and possibly sometimes not so informal, "party" of the communist revolution.

CHAPTER 5

■ VALUE, TIME, AND COMMUNISM: RE-READING MARX

This chapter is not about digging into layers of thought and balancing merit: abstract notions—work, time, labour time, and productivity—indicate what we wish to change in this world, and how.

1) The Origin of Value[1]

Capital Volume I does not begin with a definition of what capitalism is, but how it "presents itself": "an immense accumulation of commodities." This approach points to a particular choice of perspective. Marx broaches the issue with the encounter of independent producers who meet on the market to exchange their wares. Since capital/labour is the heart of the matter, as Marx himself points out, and since he is not writing a history book, why not start with the encounter of the wage-earner and the capitalist? His enquiry into wage-labour is initiated from the point of view of a division of labour between self-employed producers (farmer meets cloth-maker), and proceeds to analyse the dual nature of labour: concrete (labour has use value) and abstract (it produces exchange value).

According to Marx, use value takes up the character of exchange value once it enters the market. He describes the process as if value, instead of being born out of a very specific type of production, came *after* the productive moment and imposed itself upon work as an exterior constraint. It follows that the task of revolution would be to free the producers from this constraint.

Though Marx constantly relates value to labour, he does not insist upon its origin in *production*. Yet value results from a certain type of production, in which each item is *made for* and *according to* the labour time necessary to make it. Therefore communism as Marx sees it is a money-less world based on communal work: the trouble is, work is a lot more than people getting together in a workshop to manufacture objects. Work includes time-counting and time-saving, which in turn implies quantifying average labour time necessary to produce this or that item: in other words, what Marx rightly calls *value*. Marx treats use value like a natural result of human activity, and would like to have use values without exchange value. But use value is an analytic category both opposed to *and encompassed by* exchange value: it is impossible to do away with one without doing away with the other.

"Marx has offered much more than was directly essential for the practical conduct of the class war. . . . It is not true that Marx no longer suffices for our needs. On the contrary, our needs are not yet adequate for the utilisation of Marx's ideas."[2]

That not-so-obvious idea suggested by Rosa Luxemburg over a century ago is even more relevant than she thought. Because of the historical limits of the proletarian movement in his time, because "mankind always sets itself only such tasks as it can solve,"[3] Marx could not take his own intuitions to their ultimate conclusions. He gave all the elements to understand that value *originates* in production and *manifests* itself in exchange, but he still presented exchange—the market—as if it determined the whole process: therefore a market-less production, namely associated work, would be the key to emancipation. Hence the variations in Marx's critique of work:

2) Work Abolished, or Work as Our Prime Want?

In 1846, Marx argued that "the communist revolution is directed against the preceding mode of activity" and "does away with labour" (*German Ideology*, Part I, D).

This was a long way from identifying man as *Homo faber*, or a "toolmaker" (Benjamin Franklin).

Twenty years later, there is a shift in emphasis: "So far therefore as labour is a creator of use value, is useful labour, it is a necessary condition, independent of all forms of society, for the existence of the human race; it is an eternal nature-imposed necessity, without which there can be no material exchanges between man and Nature, and therefore no life." (*Capital*, 1867, chap. 1, 2)

Capital's first chapter regards labour (not *wage*-labour, labour *in general*) as something that has existed since the dawn of mankind and in nearly every society. As the "man and nature" metabolism becomes an object of enquiry under the category of "labour," labour turns *work* into an eternal natural fact. We are left with the idea that work, not work as we know it now, but what it may have been in very old times, before private property, before money, classes, etc., and what it could become in communism, i.e. work *without a labour market*, is positive and necessary.

The *Critique of the Gotha Programme* (1875) described "a higher phase of communist society, after the enslaving subordination of the individual to the division of labour, and therewith also the antithesis between mental and physical labour, has vanished; after labour has become not only a means of life but life's prime want; after the productive forces have also increased with the all-around development of the individual, and all the springs of co-operative wealth flow more abundantly."

Here Marx launched what was to be the ABC of Marxism: the proletarian ceases to be a proletarian (i.e. a wage-earner exploited by a boss) when everyone works. Now, *which* work? *wage*-labour? Marx proceeds as if the question was irrelevant: as soon as we all belong to the work community and there are no bourgeois, extending work to everyone solves the social question. Getting rid of capitalism is not perceived of as abolishing the capital/labour reunion, but as liberating work from capital, from its alienated prison.

In the 1840s, Marx started from a radical standpoint that was utterly unacceptable in his time (and has remained so up to now). Thirty years and a few proletarian defeats later, by labour becoming "life's prime want," he certainly meant a complete reconfiguration of creative activity. But for him, achieving this goal required more development of "the productive forces." The historical thread Marx was weaving in the 1840s proved in contradiction to the working class movement as it was really developing (unions, parties, parliamentary action, etc.). Sadly but logically, Marx's late vision remained hampered by capitalist pictures of the future: only a worker-led economic growth would ultimately free mankind.

3) Time as Measure

According to *Capital*, "In all states of society, the labour time that it costs to produce the means of subsistence, must necessarily be an object of interest to mankind, though not of equal interest in different stages of development." (Vol. I, chap. 1, 4)

The 1857–58 manuscripts (the *Grundrisse*) are reputed to be quite different from *Capital*. In many respects they are, especially because they link exploitation to alienation. Still, one can read in those pages the same contradictions as in Marx's published writings, on *work* as well as on *time*, and both concepts are indeed interlocked.

> Real economy—saving—consists of the saving of labour time (minimum, and minimization, of production costs) . . . The saving of labour time [is] equal to an increase of free time, i.e. time for the full development of the individual.[4]

> It goes without saying . . . that direct labour time itself cannot remain in the abstract antithesis to free time in which it appears from the perspective of bourgeois economy. Labour cannot become play, as Fourier would like, although it remains his great contribution to have expressed the suspension not of distribution, but of the mode of production itself, in a higher form, as the ultimate object.

True, life, and of course productive acts, require "practical use of the hands and free bodily movement," and imply effort and exertion, and we must bear this in mind, especially against the myth of automation-induced freedom. Nevertheless, the work v. play opposition is a dead-end: these are historical, not natural, categories.

Not everything can be turned into fun. Quite. But as there is a difference between production and economy, the necessity of *effort* does not mean that it has to take the form of *work*. It is not always more pleasant to eat than to cook. And what about washing up? It only becomes a chore because of the mechanical nature of housework (80 percent of which are still performed by women in Western Europe and North America), that has to be done under double pressure from time-saving and family life as we know it. Re-appropriating and altering our conditions of existence involve new relationships between man/woman, but also parent/child, adult/youth, which call for another habitat, another education, etc.

What we read in the *Grundrisse* is as profound as ambiguous:

> Capital itself is the moving contradiction, [in] that it presses to reduce labour time to a minimum, while it posits labour time, on the other side, as sole measure and source of wealth.

> The more this contradiction develops, the more does it become evident that the growth of the forces of production can no longer be boun.d up with the appropriation of alien labour, but that the mass of workers must themselves appropriate their own surplus labour. Once they have done so—and disposable time thereby ceases to have an antithetical existence—then, on one side, necessary labour time will be measured by the needs of the social individual, and, on the other, the development of the power of social production will grow so rapidly that, even though production is now calculated for the wealth of all, disposable time will grow for all.

Capitalism "is thus, despite itself, instrumental in creating the means of social disposable time, in order to reduce labour time for the whole society to a diminishing minimum, and thus to free everyone's time for their own development. But its tendency is always, on the one side, to create disposable time, on the other, to convert it into surplus labour."

"For real wealth is the developed productive power of all individuals. The measure of wealth is then not any longer, in any way, labour time, but rather disposable time."

By definition, *disposable* time has not been employed yet, is still potential, therefore impossible to measure. There is a difference between saying: "I'll work in your garden tomorrow from 2 to 4," as a *local exchange trading system* partner would say (as an interest-free credit swap, LETS *is* based on labour-time count), and saying: "I'll help you gardening tomorrow afternoon," as a friend might say. So Marx's disposable time seems to break with value. But the question remains: in a future society, will this disposable time become the totality of time, or will it be simply *added* to an always present labour-time, even reduced to a couple of hours a day? . . . Further on, Marx defines "free time" as "both idle time and time for higher activity," so we are not any wiser.

Marx posed the "time-count" issue (which is fundamental to the question of work) but could not solve it because he was addressing it on the basis of the notion of time itself.

Time is indeed the dimension of human liberation, providing the measure of time does not turn into measuring the world and us according to time.

4) Community Planning

"Let us now picture . . . a community of free individuals, carrying on their work with the means of production in common, in which the labour power of all the different individuals is consciously applied as the combined labour power of the community. . . . The total product of our community is a social product. . . . We will assume, but merely for the sake of a parallel with the production of commodities, that the share of each individual producer in the means of subsistence is determined by his labour time." (*Capital*, vol. I, chap. 1, 4)

If Marx assumes that labour time will regulate production, "merely for the sake of a parallel with the production of commodities," this is because the opposite assumption would be near unthinkable. Though this is for the sake of a comparison, his perspective is indeed to replace small private producers by social work, bourgeois rule by community rule, and anarchy and waste by democratic planning.

The whole plan hinges on transparency and self-understanding: in future, human beings will be conscious of what they do. At present, the bourgeois do not know what labour time amounts to, and they don't want to know, because an accurate reckoning of labour time would reveal the extent of the exploitation of labour. Exact opposite in communism: in Marx's view, associated producers will be able to compute the labour time necessary to whatever they manufacture.

Marx repeatedly refused to draw blueprints for the future. So it is significant that when he did elaborate on the subject in his *Critique of the Gotha Programme* (1875), his suggestion for the "lower phase" of communism, labour vouchers, amounted to *value without money*.

5) Council Communism and Labour Time

We can now address the councilist project. The gist of it originated in 1930, when the GIK (Group of Internationalist Communists of Holland) published "Fundamental Principles of Communist Production and Distribution." Jan Appel had done the first draft, and later the scheme was laid down in more details, by Paul Mattick in particular.

Its main principle is the "introduction of the Average Social Hour of Labour as a unit of economic regulation and control. . . . All money will be declared worthless and only labour certificates will give entitlement to social product. It will be possible to exchange this "certificate money" only at the cooperative shops and warehouses. The sudden abolition of money will bring about a situation in which, equally suddenly, all products must have their appropriate ASRT (Average Social Reproduction Time) stamped upon them."[5]

Now, if the GIK gave a key role to labour time counting, it was not from an economist's or a technician's point of view, because that method would be more efficient or better adapted to modern industry. In a short autobiographical note, in 1966, Jan Appel made it clear what the idea that underpinned the plan was:

> the most profound and intense contradiction in human society resides in the fact that . . . the right of decision over the conditions of production, over what and how much is produced and in what quantity, is taken away from the producers themselves and placed in the hands of highly centralised organs of power. . . . This basic division in human society can only be overcome when the producers finally assume their right of control over the conditions of their labour, over what they produce and how they produce it. . . . It was likewise a wholly new conception to concentrate one's attention . . . upon the exercise of power by the factory organisations, the Workers' Councils, in their assumption of control over the factories and places of work; in order that flowing from this, the unit of the average social hour of labour, as the measure of the production times of all goods and services in both production and distribution, might be introduced.[6]

This highlights the prime purpose of the scheme: to make sure all producers would be able to understand how production functions, so they can take authentic collective decisions. Nobody else but the producers is in the best position to know what production implies in terms of material and human resources, and the only way of synthesising all productive factors is to reduce them to their common denominator: human labour, measured in time, ASRT, the great and fair simplifier. So it will be necessary to "adopt as the nodal point of all economic activity the duration of labour time expended in the production of all use values, as the equivalent measure replacing money values, and around which the whole of economic life would revolve."

As seen above in sections 1 and 3, Marx was in contradiction with himself when he presented social labour time as something different from and opposed to value, but his notes did not elaborate the idea into a full definitive plan. Council communism's ASRT brings this contradiction to a stage where it is untenable:

The bourgeois does not know what *value* is: he only bothers about *profit*, *interest*, or *rent*, and when economists discuss value, it is these three forms they are talking about, not Marxian value. Yet, according to council communists, the associated producers would be able to evaluate the individual and the collective physical-mental energy necessary to produce objects, and to measure that exertion in time. This is forgetting that labour time, because it is a social average, is hardly computable for a specific task or object. Value *does* exist, but not as a management technique instrument.

The money-less utopia goes a long way: whereas money is the natural tool of the rich, the common people want a standard that comes from them, from those who do the real thing, who create riches. After all, any effort can be reduced to a certain exertion measurable in time (considering the intensity of the task and skill involved). In order to expand "free" time, the aim is to locate "working hours" and reduce them as much as possible.[7]

Council communists proposed a proletarian variation on that theme. To avoid utopia, the plan starts from three postulates: production has to be done, cannot be turned into play, and its process is so complex that it requires planning. The labour time-based economy meets all three requisites. It would make worker management possible and exploitation impossible: gold, coins, or notes can be accumulated to hire labour; labour-time vouchers can't. Besides, a labour time-based economy would eliminate waste and reconcile fairness with efficiency.

A 1994 essay describes "a society based on labour time": "The only way time can become 'free' is by making the products of that time free as well. The products of our work can all be compared with one another in terms of the time taken or spent producing them. So now we can, if we choose, suppress prices, markets, and so on and make distribution of all products 'free' in exchange for the 'time' of the producers ... Only when the producers themselves know the true costs of production can they take control of or manage the production process."[8]

In such plans, in spite of complete political and economic worker democracy, *work* is not abolished as such, as something distinct from the rest of life.

For the GIK, the company explicitly stood as an economic unit at the centre of the system. Of course, council communists were aware of the inescapable fact that some companies, and some workers within each company, would be more productive than others: they thought this would be compensated for by a complex regulating mechanism detailed by Mattick.[9] However, if the regulator is labour time, this entails the imperative of being productive, and productivity is no servant: it rules over production. The shop floor would soon lose control over its elected supervisors, and democratically designated co-organisers would act as bosses. The system of councils would survive as an illusion, and workers' management result in capitalism, or rather ... capitalism would never have disappeared. We can't have it both ways: either we keep the foundation of value, or we dispense with it. The circle can't be squared.

Such a scheme goes as close as one can get to keeping the essentials of capitalism yet putting them under full worker control.

6) Bordiga's Critique

The GIK and Pannekoek's vision was born as a counterpoint to Leninist and then Stalinist Russia, and owed a lot to a prevailing mood created by the 1930s Depression. Across the political spectrum, Otto Rühle, Bruno Rizzi, dissident Trotskyists Burnham and Schachtman, non-Marxists Berle and Means, and many others thought capitalism was on its way to planning, bureaucratisation, and nationalisation. During the war, Joseph Schumpeter announced the end of the age of private entrepreneurs, and for him the question was whether a new socialised economy would come under democratic or dictatorial rule.[10] After 1945, this perception was reinforced by the growing power of the USSR and Mao's victory in China. Socialisme ou Barbarie is now well-known as an eminent theorist of world bureaucratisation, but similar views were common at the time. Karl Korsch wrote in 1950:

> The control of the workers over the production of their own lives will not come from their occupying the positions, on the international and world markets, abandoned by the self-destroying and so-called free competition of the monopolistic owners of the means of production. This control can only result from a planned intervention by all the classes today excluded from it into a production which today is already tending in every way to be regulated in a monopolistic and planned fashion.[11]

For council communists, the revolutionary question became how labour could take over the management of a more and more "organised" capitalism and thereby transform it in a socialist/communist economy. Russia played the part of a counter-model. To quote one of the editions of the GIK's text, the objective was that "once the workers have won power through their mass organisations," they "will be able to hold on to that power."

Bordiga stood apart because he refused the concept of "bureaucracy" as a new social agent which would play in the twentieth century an epochal role comparable to the bourgeoisie before. (Please, reader, bear with me, this detour is no divagation, rather a Situationist-like drift with a purpose.)

Our "Crash Course" (chapter 3) mentioned Bordiga's constant pro-Lenin stand (though his theory of the party differed from Lenin's). Such persistency paradoxically helped him grasp the nature of capitalism and of communism. The main reason why it took him so long to analyse Russia as capitalist and the Comintern as anti-revolutionary, is for him the bureaucracy/rank and file opposition was never a key issue. He rejected the theory of "bureaucratic" capitalism: the Russian command economy run by the party-State did not differ in nature from Western bourgeois-led capitalism. The enigma was not the bureaucracy, but the essential economic laws which the bureaucracy had to obey, and he saw these laws as described in *Capital*: value accumulation, exchange of commodities, declining rate of profit, etc. Only relative backwardness prevented Russia from the "usual" manifestations of over-production, which asserted itself anyhow, particularly by waste. During the Cold War, when many a council communist depicted bureaucratic regimes as the likely future of capitalist evolution, Bordiga foresaw that the U.S. dollar would penetrate Russia, and ultimately crack the Kremlin walls.

The German-Dutch left was right to define the USSR as capitalist: the reason why it defined it as capitalist was flawed. Because there were no private bourgeois, no privately owned business and because competition seemed inexistent, council communists believed that Stalin's Russia had altered at least some of the fundamentals set down by Marx.[12] It insisted on the control of the economy by the bureaucracy, to which it opposed the slogan of worker management. Bordiga said there was no need for a new programme: worker management is a secondary matter, and workers will only be able to manage the economy if market and value relations are abolished.

The debate goes far beyond the analysis of bureaucratic or State capitalism.

Because wage-labour and value were essential to Bordiga's definition of capitalism, he better understood what the USSR was. At the same time, as he dismissed the bureaucratic or State capitalist theories, he missed the bureaucratic issue, which is a real one, not in the German-Dutch sense which gives it pre-eminence, but in the sense that there will be no revolution without proletarian self-action. "The proletarian movement is the *self-conscious*, *independent* movement of the *immense majority*, in the interest of the immense majority" (*Communist Manifesto*, chap. 1: our emphasis). The German-Dutch left was among the few who took these words seriously. In short, Bordiga thought communism could be achieved top down. Councilism prioritised worker democracy (and some like Castoriadis, in the end, just democracy). Bordiga prioritised dictatorship. However, his consistency in defining communism neither as a matter of consciousness nor as a matter of management remains valid and essential.

7) Does Value Abolish Itself?

One more episode in the value saga . . .

If revolution is a complete break with capitalism, this raises the question of what causes it. The proletariat makes the revolution, no doubt, but Marx often presents proletarian action as a side-effect of industrialisation, as if the development of productive forces not only contributed to revolution, but was its major *cause*. This is what Marx suggests in relation to the first automated machines, with special reference to computing pioneer Charles Babbage:

> As the basis on which large industry rests, the appropriation of alien labour time, ceases, with its development, to make up or to create wealth, so does direct labour as such cease to be the basis of production, since, in one respect, it is transformed more into a supervisory and regulatory activity; but then also because the product ceases to be the product of isolated direct labour, and the combination of social activity appears, rather, as the producer. (*Grundrisse*: see note 4)

> As soon as labour in the direct form has ceased to be the great well-spring of wealth, labour time ceases and must cease to be its measure, and hence exchange value [must

cease to be the measure] of use value. . . . With that, production based on exchange value breaks down, and the direct, material production process is stripped of the form of penury and antithesis.

In other words, when it becomes impossible to trace the personal contribution of an individual worker to wealth creation, the law of value (the regulation of production and circulation of goods by the amount of average labour time necessary to produce them) hinders economic progress and mutates into an absurdity which triggers historical change.

In the past, the growing merchant power had exploded feudal shackles and replaced aristocratic rule with bourgeois rule. Soon the industrial thrust, the economic socialisation and the concentrated masses of workers would prove incompatible with private property and bourgeois domination. Proletarian revolution was thought of on the model of democratic bourgeois revolution. The author of *Capital* partook of his time's belief in historical progress, and added a revolutionary twist: capitalist development led to communism.

Marx cannot be simplified into this position, but there is enough in his work to warrant it. Present in his analysis is the tension of the time of bourgeois triumph. "Social labour" implies the possibility of rejecting all forms of alienated practice, but the concept oscillated between utopia in the 1840s and practical politics in later years. At about the same time as the *Grundrisse*, he was writing that

At a certain stage of development, the material productive forces of society come into conflict with the existing relations of production. . . . From forms of development of the productive forces these relations turn into their fetters. Then begins an era of social revolution. The changes in the economic foundation lead sooner or later to the transformation of the whole immense superstructure. (preface to his *Contribution to a Critique of Political Economy*, published in 1859)

As explained in the conclusion of *Capital* volume I, "capitalist production begets, with the inexorability of a law of Nature, its own negation. It is the negation of negation."

This "expropriation of a few usurpers by the mass of the people" will be possible when capitalist development (= the development of productive forces) renders useless and absurd the coexistence of exploiting and exploited classes. The *Grundrisse* expounds the same dialectic: "As the system of bourgeois economy has developed for us only by degrees, so too its negation, which is its ultimate result."

Many a thinker (their name is legion) has taken pains to demonstrate how the "law of value" was tending to abolish itself (the word *law* is typical of the decline of critique into science). These theorists herald the advent of a time when the average social labour time would mutate into an inadequate measuring rod and ineffective regulator. Sooner or later, wage-labour's own socialisation would tear the system apart as an outmoded frame.

This amounts to revolutionary change without revolution.

No. There is no tipping point when the wage-labour system would render itself null and void. Let us not expect capitalist contradictions to solve those of the proletariat, because the proletariat also *is* a contradiction: it is situated both at the inner heart and outside of capitalism. Theories of (violent or gradual) capital self-destruction dodge this contradiction, which has to do with class struggle. In particular, as no expenditure of physical or mental effort can be accurately broken down to seconds and minutes, complete submission of labour by capital is impossible. The proletarians' fight against capital is based on their resistance to what the bourgeois turns them into: an activity bound in and forced into productive time.

8) Marx as a Marxist

In order to distinguish between Marx and his many non-revolutionary successors, radicals have often contended that Marx himself was the first and probably best critique of Marxism. (I did it too.)

Sometimes the road to a mistake is paved with good intentions.

As soon as "Marxism" emerged, Marxists started looking over Marx's writings to find the demonstration that one day capitalist socialisation would prevent capitalism from perpetuating itself. This might be a good definition of Marxism, actually: replacing proletarian action by fairly peaceful evolution or by a beneficial catastrophe, but in any case a quasi-natural process. At the end of the nineteenth century, this structural limit was perceived in the contradiction between bourgeois property and such a huge productive blossoming that even cartels and trusts would be incapable of mastering it. As volumes II and III of *Das Kapital* came out, they were read as proof that enlarged reproduction of capital would inevitably reach breaking point.

Nowadays, the analysis shifts from the economic to the social crisis, and from the worker to the people as an agent of change. Thanks to the 1857–58 manuscripts being available,[13] the limitation is now said to be in the contemporary sources of wealth, which supposedly exceed so much capitalist structure that they call for its suppression, like a fabric bursting at the seams. Toni Negri will not be the last one to read in the *Grundrisse* that value (the regulation of production by labour time, by the hunt for minimal production cost) is already ceasing to rule modern society: according to Negri, the world now depends on the *general* or *social intellect*.[14] All we (a *we* likely to include about 99 percent of the population) would have to do is grow aware of this historical discrepancy, turn potential evolution into effective change, and society would be transformed.

In plain English, in the twenty-first century as in 1900, productive forces are portrayed as if they were antagonistic to value and wage-labour, and on the verge of spiralling out of bourgeois control.

This interpretation is biased but, as explained before, not unfaithful to Marx's letter and spirit.

There is more to it than simply contrasting young Marx to the old. Contradictions abounded in (and *drove forward*) his writings from beginning to end. He followed a consistent and discontinued path from the 1840s unpublished manuscripts to the (often equally unpublished) manuscripts of later years. In the 1860s, at the same time as he was having far-reaching insights in what is known as the *Grundrisse*, he was never-finishing his masterwork, *Capital*. The title is significant of Marx's priority: a twenty- or thirty-year effort to immerse himself in the ins and outs of capitalism in order to understand its possible overthrow. The means turned into an end: the more he wanted to get to the essentials of the proletariat, the deeper he went into studying capitalism. Procrastination is often a sign that problem and solution are indissolubly mixed.

Undoubtedly, we criticise Marx with the help of Marx, and the most enlightening comment remains the one Bordiga made more than fifty years ago: Marxian texts have to be read as a "description of the features of communist society." That being said, what dominated Marx's life and work? Not only did he leave his literally blinding intuitions aside, but even those insights mixed the supersession of the economy with the project of a community economy (see section 4 above). Marx is more a critic of money and commodity than of work and productivity. If he gave a minor place to a communist revitalisation of the Russian peasant commune compared to worldwide industrialisation, it was because capitalist headway went along with an ascending worker movement which was essential to him.[15]

"The free trade system is destructive. It breaks up old nationalities and pushes the antagonism of the proletariat and the bourgeoisie to the extreme point. In a word, the free trade system hastens the social revolution. It is in this revolutionary sense alone, gentlemen, that I vote in favour of free trade."[16]

We cannot set ourselves free from the limits of the period we happen to live in, and we are as time-bound as Marx and Engels were.

Understanding communism implies distinguishing Marx from Marxism *without* denying the link between the two. Otherwise, we would risk making up Marx in accordance to our wishes, or (worse) with the winds of time. We can already read about a Marx who was an ecologist before ecology. Maybe soon we will be told about an esoteric Marx who theorised gender.

CHAPTER 6

■ THE BITTER VICTORY OF COUNCILISM

Needless to say, the "victory" we speak of here is not the sort of achievement that past and present councilists were and are aiming at: only a sad, unavoidable ideological victory. Ideology is not necessarily made of false data, nor does it put forward only wrong ideas. It is a deformed consciousness of reality (and therefore usually incorporates hard facts), which provides people with a way of understanding history and themselves in it.

Councilism is a mental mapping born as much out of proletarian endeavours as out of their limits. While worker self-organisation was (and remains) necessary, it was (and is) not enough to overthrow capitalism. Instead of perceiving this limit for what it is—a limit—ideology sets it as the objective of the movement. Ideologisation is the process by which the whole of proletarian history is re-interpreted as if this limitation was its essence. Councilism is worker councils turned into the be-all-and-end-all of revolution.

Like any other partial truth, it has fallen prey to "recuperation." The ability of modern society to integrate and digest radical critique is nothing new, or to be afraid of. Nowadays, because capitalism carries the day, as long as the essentials (private property, wage-labour, the authority of the State) are respected, the allowed margin of freedom is larger than before, and we are granted lots of "discursive space." I once saw graffiti on a white wall in Vienna:

← freedom from here to here →

Not only is "law and order" compatible with innocuous critique and inoffensive social experiment, it also needs our active involvement in the day-to-day running of society. In democratic countries, providing you pay the rent, you're free to extol Buddha or Bakunin. "Changing things so everything stays the same," as Giuseppe Tomasi di Lampedusa wrote in *The Leopard*. Traditional "bourgeois" culture has gone multicultural and nonconformity is marketed. More harmless personal freedom, more leeway, more community watch, more peer-control too. The most modern aspects of contemporary discourse have renounced a strict hierarchy, and see no contradiction in promoting at the same time individualism (self-empowerment) and collective values (the team spirit).

"Self-empowerment in its simplest form means taking charge of your own life, in your work place, with your colleagues, with your subordinates, with your superiors, with your body, with your illness and for you caring for yourself" (Self-Empowerment & Development Centre, 2013).

As a result, a consensus has emerged on the virtues of *autonomy*: peer assessment in the classroom, power-sharing and self-governance for local associations and public bodies, management by agreed-upon objectives in the office, horizontalism in the Occupy and the Squares movements, autonomous space for alternativists in many cities, etc. Parliamentarianism is aging, let's revive it with strong doses of participatory or monitory democracy.[1] Communal goal-setting, self-development, and networking make the news. Leninist party builders are a joke. Party-ism is down, grass-roots-ism prevails.

Secondly, "*information* first" has become part of dominant ideology: maximum and fastest information! The assumption is the more we know, the more we understand, but above all we need *facts*, and correct understanding will comes from lots of data: "Knowing is Doing." Mainstream society is obsessed with education and empowerment: community civic classes (learning to be a community-minded citizen) now extends to global civics (learning to be ecologically concerned).

This universal trend is unfortunately reflected in the radical milieu. ICO (and now Echanges & Mouvement) claimed to have no theory except the theory that only the proletarians could determine their own methods and aims. Likewise, thousands of infokiosks and indymedia collectives profess to have no specific doctrine (Marxist, anarchist, ecologist, feminist, whatever) and say their sole purpose is to serve as a meeting place and communication centre meant to promote social struggles, with the difference that the "historical subject" is no longer the working class, but the people (the famous 99%). They act as if ICO's "choice of non-existence" (*IS* no. 11) had been inverted into the choice of 24/7 online presence, yet *information first* remains the priority, too often with similar features as "bourgeois" media: constant data flow, information overload and obsolescence, sensationalism . . . Radicality is reduced to a description and exaltation of manifold struggles.

The autonomy principle and the information fascination can best be seen at work in the world wide web: the Internet is the universal dispenser, accelerator, and multiplier of data and ideas. The "chattering classes" have expanded far beyond the readership of the *Guardian* or the *New York Times*: everyone is an opinion giver and receiver now. For those who believe that social change will come out of ever more global knowledge and discussion, cyber-activism is ideal. A planetary critical sub-society is waging a permanent war of the words.

This is all happening in the realm of ideology. In reality, we do not live in a bottom-up society. Far from it. Nineteenth-century *factory despotism* has not gone. Today's boss tells you what to do and punishes you if you misbehave, and not just in dictatorial China. In Amazon's European warehouses, the company lords over the life of its labour force to the point of telling employees how to park their cars: trespassing over the white line separating the parking spaces gets you a "warning." And democratic America offers a wide range of societal and cultural arch-conservatives who manage to put back the cultural societal clock.

So, as far as ideas matter, a mere ideological victory, miles away from Anton Pannekoek's writings or ultra-leftist summer camps. At the end of the nineteenth century, Marxism watered-down Marx to an apologist of worker productivism. Later, hundreds of millions were oppressed in his name, and North Koreans still are. More recently, Debord has been transmogrified into an anti-art artist: he no longer has a "bad reputation." Amadeo Bordiga would prove too much to chew for acamedic pundits, but who knows? The old Neapolitan's insights on ecology, his cutting sharp-worded style and scathing wit could add a much-wanted provocative flavour to current discourse. There is no doctrine that infotainment is unable to feed on. No-one is innocent. Everybody is liable to prosecution or recuperation.

The German-Dutch left indeed had a strong point in 1920 and later, when it rejected the mass parties of the Second and Third Internationals in the name of radical worker self-activity. The conundrum was that the call for *worker power* conflicted with the communist perspective of the *abolition of work*, when only the abolition of work could get rid of capitalism. In 1920, the proletarians stood at the crossroads, stayed there, did not meet the challenge that their own uprising had created, and were defeated. As the perspective of going beyond work and the commodity had hardly emerged in the 1920s or '30s, and only began to assert itself in the '60s, the contradiction was inevitable at the time and lingered on in the way the radical minority could understand itself. Recuperation always feeds on such inner contradictions, by prioritising some aspects of theory and deflecting others.

"Recuperation" is the normal process by which society recovers parts of what tried to negate it, so there is nothing here to reproach councilists with. What is objectionable, though, is a persistent failure to realise how and why such a specific ideologising diversion could take place. Some basic councilist tenets have been incorporated within dominant ideas, because they were based on historical limits, and it is these limits that we must comprehend. Ideology only trivialises and sterilises theoretical aspects by separating theory from the practice where it originated.

"The emancipation of the working classes must be conquered by the working classes themselves." These were the Rules of the International Workingmen's Association, approved by its Geneva congress in 1866. Autonomy is indispensable, not just to initiate revolution, also to accomplish it: who else but the self-organising proletarians could do away with the proletariat? But it's not enough. It is not the principle on which everything can or must be based. Autonomy means giving oneself one's own law (*nomos*). It's based on the self (*auto*). As far as the proletarians are concerned, what *self* are we talking about? Praising worker autonomy is mistaking the part for the whole, fragment of a frozen totality.

The same obviously applies to the most recuperated of all, Karl Marx: we cannot be content with repeating that the *dictatorship of the proletariat* he wrote about had absolutely nothing in common with Trotsky's militarisation of labour or Stalin's Five Year Plan. As we hope to have shown in the previous chapter, there is no point for us reading Marx unless we care to see how much he owed to his time.

CHAPTER 7

■ POSTLUDE

> "When you have eliminated the impossible,
> whatever remains, *however improbable*,
> must be the truth." (*The Sign of the Four*, 1890)

Three editions in forty years. Not much to be proud of. When radical critique is republished, it is proof that a whole generation (author included) failed to achieve the overall change that generation was aiming at. It also reminds us that revolution is not made by books, magazines, leaflets, or online postings: words are blank bullets.

New editions are only a good omen if writer and reader understand how much the republished texts were relevant ... and still are. In our case, this implies some appraising of the current situation. The Black & Red (1974) and the Antagonism (1998) editions contained prefaces dealing with periods as different from each other as both were from the present situation. The contemporary crisis is probably deeper than that of the 1970s, but more difficult to grasp.

1) Revolutionary Optimism and Historical Determinism

Our 1973 belief that "counter-revolution is finally coming to a close, a new movement is rising ..." was clearly mistaken. In fact, what followed the 1970s is hardly comparable with the interwar counter-revolution, because there was no serious insurrectionary attempt in the '60s and '70s, so in spite of bloodshed and repression, in Latin America and Asia particularly, Western and Japanese capitalism could afford to be less violently anti-revolutionary than in the days of Hitler and Stalin.

Such a sequence of events is enough to cast doubt on a determinist undercurrent that flows through some parts of this book that were written in the early '70s. This raises the question of why and how radicals are tempted to turn history into a pre-conditioned one-way road to revolution:

> It is not a question of what this or that proletarian, or even the whole proletariat, at the moment regards as its aim. It is a question of what the proletariat is, and what, in accordance with this being, it will historically be compelled to do. Its aim and historical action is visibly and irrevocably foreshadowed in its own life situation as well as in the whole organisation of bourgeois society today. There is no need to explain here that a large part of the English and French proletariat is already conscious of its historic task and is constantly working to develop that consciousness into complete clarity (*The Holy Family*, IV, 4, Critical comment no. 2).

This was written in 1844: we now know that the last sentence did not agree with facts. But there is more here than meets the eye. Marx and Engels wished to distance themselves from utopians (who relied on consciousness, morals, or the generosity of bourgeois kind enough to finance their dreamland schemes), as well as from reformists (who hoped for gradual evolution). On the contrary, Marx and Engels contended that, however weak, defeated, or non-revolutionary the proletarians may be, their success was rooted in the implacable condition that capital forced upon labour:

Capitalism → Communism

More than a century later, radicals like us would take up this quote and similar ones as ammunition against Leninist party-building, and against activism: trying to give history a push. We wished to stress that the proletarians do more than resist exploitation and oppression: they have an inner ability to self-organise and eventually revolutionise the wage-labour and statist world into communism, *because* their condition itself carries this possibility.

Presenting a possibility as a historical necessity always contains the risk of cultivating a mapped-out vision, as if the proletariat were fulfilling a destiny, as if we were prophets of the ultimate meaning of history: determinism is teleology for the materialist. The formula

Capitalism → Proletariat → Communism

is only valid if the middle term acts revolutionary. Communist theory has certainty of purpose, not of success (see below, sections 3 and 5).

2) What Heritage Do We Renounce?

We have seen in chapter 5 that Marx's analysis of value was open to dispute. More generally, how does the vision of people like Marx relate to social-democrat watered-down Marxism, and to the monstrosities that labelled themselves "communist" in the twentieth century?

In the late 1960s and in the '70s, "going back to Marx" was imperative if we wished to understand what we were experiencing.[1] Our return to revolutionary history included the left opposition to the Third International (the "Italian" and "German-Dutch" lefts), but also pre- and post-1914 anarchism. Contrary to Marx's 1872 anti-Bakunin pamphlet (one of his weakest writings[2]), a *veritable split* happened in the mid-nineteenth century within the revolutionary movement between what became stultified as Marxism and anarchism. Later of course the split got worse. As readers can see for themselves, we are not adding little bits of Bakunin to big chunks of Marx: we are only trying to assess both Marx and Bakunin as Marx and Bakunin themselves had to assess, say, Babeuf or Fourier.

There was a progressivist dimension in Marx: he shared the nineteenth century's belief in evolution as a succession of logically necessary steps on the way to a happy future, with the certainty that today was better than yesterday, and tomorrow surely brighter. He held a linear view of history, and built up a deterministic continuity from primitive community to communism, which can be summed up like this:

In early history, when human groups were able to produce more than was necessary for immediate survival, this surplus created the possibility of exploitation: a minority forced the majority to work and grabbed the riches. Thousands of years later, thanks to capitalist industrialisation, the huge expansion of productivity makes the end of exploitation possible. Goods are so plentiful that it becomes absurd to have a minority monopolise them. And production is so socialised that it becomes pointless (and counterproductive) to have it run by a handful of rulers each managing his own private business. The bourgeois were historically necessary: now their own achievement (modern economic growth) turns them into parasites. Capitalism makes itself useless.

True, such an intellectual pattern was never actually written down by Marx, but it is the underlying logic beneath a lot of his texts and (what's more important) a lot of his political activity. It was no accident or mistake if he tactically supported the German national bourgeoisie and was often tolerant of openly reformist union or party leaders: he regarded them as agents of the positive change that would eventually bring about communism. By contrast, he looked down on such insurrectionists as Bakunin whom he thought stood outside the *real* movement of history.

Though the deterministic Marx was not the whole Marx, who showed a long-standing interest in what did not fit within the linear succession of historical phases, Marxism was born as the ideology of economic development: if capitalism gets more and more socialised, there's little need for revolution: the organised masses will eventually put a (mainly peaceful) end to bourgeois anarchy. In sum, socialism does not break with capitalism: it completes it. Radicals only differed from gradualists in that they added the necessity of violence to the process. In *Imperialism: The Highest Stage of Capitalism* (1916), Lenin made much of the fact that big German *konzerns* and cartels were already organised and centralised from the top: if bourgeois managers were replaced by working class ones, and this rational planning was extended from each private trust to the whole of industry, the general social fabric would be altered. This was no breakaway from the commodity and the economy. Any economic definition of communism remains within the scope of the economy, i.e. the separation of productive time-space from the rest of life.

3) "Class": What Class?
Defining class and proletariat appeared fairly simple in 1848:

> The lower strata of the middle class—the small trades-people, shopkeepers, and retired tradesmen generally, the handicraftsmen and peasants—all these sink gradually into the proletariat. . . . Thus the proletariat is recruited from all classes of the population. . . . The other classes decay and finally disappear in the face of modern industry; the proletariat is its special and essential product. (*Communist Manifesto*, chap. 1)

As early as the end of the nineteenth century, revolutionary activity ran into an unanticipated problem when capitalist development proved a long way from creating an overwhelming worker mass that would gradually absorb most other classes and incorporate them into a compact whole ready to fight for socialism.

As we know, after 1917, the vast majority of the working class did not act in a revolutionary way.

When Hermann Gorter put the failure of German revolution after 1918 down to the social and political (dead)weight of the petit-bourgeois, his explanation was perfectly coherent with his vision of revolution. For him, as for most communists and a lot of anarchists at the time, revolution was the logical ultimate consequence of the growth of the toiling masses within a capitalist system which they were going to overthrow and replace by a community of associated producers.[3]

This is giving too much credit to the middle classes: the relevant question is what gave them the capacity to stand in the way of proletarian action. In post-1919 Germany, when Gorter stressed the loneliness of the proletariat, by which he meant industrial workers, he was acknowledging the inability of the revolutionary to offer to the clerk, shopkeeper, or small farmer a better future under socialism other than to become a factory worker. In Germany, Gorter wrote in 1920, "the proletariat stands alone."[4] Limiting the revolution to work and to the worker was making a virtue of necessity. The insurgent workers had been incapable of achieving what the bourgeois have done: in the nineteenth century, and to a lesser extent in the twentieth, the bourgeoisie has been able "to represent its interest as the common interest of all the members of society . . . to give its ideas the form of universality, and represent them as the only rational, universally valid ones. The class making a revolution appears from the very start . . . not as a class but as the representative of the whole of society." (*German Ideology*, 1845–46, part 1, B)

On the contrary, most of the time, the proletarian movement identified with and acted as a *worker* movement, and this is one of the reasons why it failed.

Only in its sharpest and deepest moments was the labour movement capable of going at least partially beyond the issue of labour, of becoming multi-dimensional, and logically it was at those peak-times that it proved the strongest against capital and State: to give just a few Eurocentric examples, the Paris Commune, some aspects of the October Revolution, Germany 1919–21, Spain in the 1930s . . .

History has turned the page now. We still live in an industrial society, but everyone does not work in a factory, and, although half of all Earthlings are now towns-people, revolution will not be achieved without the two or three billions of "semi-proletarians" (those "without reserve," a lot of whom are semi-rural)—let alone against them. As they communise, the proletarians will change their own condition by *also* bringing along and involving those few billions without whom there will be no change. Communisation will neither be a class dictatorship nor a class alliance. The proletarians will transform themselves at the same time as they will transform other groups. Communisation will destroy and create. It will reject and bring together. There is no point in counter-posing the workers as a bloc against the rest, as Gorter theorised it.

Nearly a hundred years have passed since the post-1917 workers' insurrections.

Until the two or three last decades of the twentieth century, most radical critique considered the working class as the social pivot and revolutionary lever (metaphors highly revealing of a mechanical age mindset). Nowadays, in contrast with the apparent simplicity of yesteryears, capitalism and contemporary struggles are said to be devoid of centrality. When most radicals speak of *labour*, they tend to overstretch the notion, with no significant difference between a house-wife, a student and an assembly-line worker. The definition has moved from entirely positive to entirely negative: the prole is no longer the pan-creator of wealth, he or she is a less-person: jobless, landless, powerless, propertyless, moneyless, homeless, and undocumented. As result, what is meant by *class* is a boundless shapeless whole, disjointed not only from the work place (which would stick to the Marxian definition: proles are at work *and/or jobless*), but from the world of work altogether.

This is disregarding the fact that the present world is structured by the capital/wage labour relation, even more so in the twenty-first century than the nineteenth. Work has not become inessential. We do not live in an un-structured com-modified totality which everybody would be equally active in reproducing: the postal worker, the psychologist, the school-girl doing her homework, the forklift driver, the couple going to a show, the lawyer busy shopping . . . Society has a *centre*: production, viz. value production, more precisely surplus-value production, and first of all the production of material objects, be they T-shirts, tablets, or a VOD film bought online. This is the main point, not the proportion of factory workers in the working population, nor the evolution from an indus-trial to a service society.

The question is not simply to have clerks barricading the streets along factory workers, or how to connect Brazilian *favelas* with Chinese industrial neighbourhoods, because if each group carries on *only* its own specific fight, the addition won't add up. Extending a workplace confined "class" to a quasi-universal "people" is no solution. A mere juxtaposition of urban riots, strikes, occupied squares, ecological activism, indigenous resistance, with no cross-fertilisation between these categories, with no attempt to do away with value production, to abolish work, to destroy State power, would accomplish no more than past "class alliances" (workers + farmers + intellectuals + . . .). A catch-all coalition of the deprived won't do any better than a workers' bloc. The issue goes deeper than the *personnel* of the revolution.

Neither should we be looking for safety in numbers.

No-one denies that there are fewer factory workers in Western Europe, North America, and Japan than in 1960. Still, let us not be believe that in the old industrial countries, everybody is now teaching, standing behind a shop counter, typing on a keyboard, communicating, programming . . . or living on the dole. Contemporary modern society is not divided between an ever-larger middle class and an ever poorer dwindling ex-working class. It is no accident that the notion of an *underclass* became popular at the same time as the notion of a *class society* fell out of fashion: whereas the working class was feared as (and was indeed) an agent of historical change, the under-class is thought of as a sad remnant of a defunct past, to be dealt with by welfare and riot police. The fading away of the proletarians is not documented by facts. In France, manual work and menial office work—jobs held by what can be called "proles"—account for about 60 percent of the working population. Besides, in the past, very few countries (Britain and Germany, for instance) ever had a majority of factory workers.

Statistics, however, do not tell the whole story. The proportion of workers is not a factor to be dismissed, but the big change resides elsewhere. For the last thirty years, west European, American, and Japanese labour has ceased to exert a major pressure on capital. This is not because they would have lost their economic function, but because they were defeated after their non-revolutionary yet militant struggle between 1960 and 1980. Indeed, it is because labour was defeated (on the shop floor and in the street) that the bourgeois were able to outsource and transfer a lot of the manufacturing. Hong Kong capitalists and mainland Chinese bureaucrats did not force their way into Western markets: Asia only became (some of) the workshops of the world after the Western and Japanese workers had lost out in the 1960s–70s. But the game is not over.

The problem is not that in Canada or Italy the proles would now have *more* than "their chains to lose," because they would be caught up in consumption and credit, and be therefore "integrated" into capitalism, whereas in Bangladesh or China the proles would have *only* their chains to lose and would therefore fit in with the *Communist Manifesto*'s definition of the revolutionary proletariat. Berlin metalworkers in 1919 enjoyed a "better" life than Lancashire textile workers in 1850, yet they rebelled against the bosses and the State. In Europe or the United States as in Asia today, the problem is the possible junction between protected labour and precarious labour, between "privileged" workers and overexploited workers. Revolution can only happen as a combination of a reaction against capitalist-induced misery and of a reaction against the riches sold by this same capitalism. Communist revolution is a joint rejection of the *worst* actually imposed by capitalism and of the *best* it offers and wants us to dream about. This fusion supposes a social context where the two types of reality, misery and wealth, coexist and face each other, so that the proletarians can attack both. This is more likely to coalesce in Denver than in Kinshasa or Dubai, or in Shanghai than in the remote corner of a Chinese province where commodity and wage-labour have not yet turned society into full-fledged capitalist relationships. (That does not mean that rural or so-called "backward" areas are further from communism than "modern" ones. In some ways, they might well be closer: as the money world has penetrated them less, they will have less to get rid of. See chap. 1, section 10).

Short and sweet, if we suppose, as we do, that communist revolution means the abolition of work as such, of the economy as such, of private property, of wage-labour, which implies the destruction of the State, some proletarians have more impact on society than others: a rail worker strike has more social leverage than a media worker strike. Yet communisation will not be achieved or "led" by factory-workers. Workers will not question work on their own: as far as we can learn from the past, nothing serious would have happened in Italy in the 1970s without mass factory stoppages, *and* factory-workers would not have started questioning wage-labour and work without a large deep unrest—outside the workplace—that went beyond labour issues. In those days as now, in-between categories (school-kids, casual labour, etc.), which are unstable, volatile, and more prone to rebellion, often facilitate radicalisation. Sociological barriers are divisive. Only interaction and mutual change will enable categories to overpass their respective limits by dealing with the heart of the matter. Only then will all (now distinct) dimensions converge. Otherwise the proletarians will be defeated if they fight as a collage of categories.

4) Surge

The current revival of worker militancy in Asia is not dissimilar from what François Martin described in chapter 2, the frequency of wildcatting particularly. However, (re)inventing forms of struggle does not necessarily provide a radically new content and perspective. As Eric Hobsbawm pointed out, rioting can be a form of collective bargaining: what the historian wrote about the Luddites can be applied to modern factory workers as well as to disenfranchised groups.[5] The development of direct and bottom-up action is a symptom of a worldwide crisis in the established political and trade-union channels, yet we see mainly negative signs of anti-capitalism, and this non-acceptance disrupts the existing order with few attempts to create a new world. The undeniable fact that the unions have hardly real wind in their sails is not enough to create a qualitatively different proletarian movement.[6]

Up to now, the new cycle of struggles does not go beyond the limit of collective bargaining by whatever means available ("peacefully if we can, forcibly if we must," the Chartists used to say), even when there is little to bargain.

The highest level of 1960s and '70s radicalism could be summed up in one word: *autonomy*, i.e. the rejection of all mediations (State, union, party, or ideology) by a militant proletarian minority, which tried to act outside and against mediators. Thirty-five or forty years after the zenith of Italian *autonomia*, autonomy has become the smallest common denominator of most social movements: grassroots action, collective decision-making, maximum information circulation. With the 1999 Seattle riot, the new "struggle cycle" picked up where the former one had left off. Unfortunately, although self-activity is indeed a *sine qua non* component of the communist movement, it is never enough to create its content.

Let us put forward two hypotheses:

[1] If the signs we perceive are anything to go by, while the proletarians of the old industrial countries are fighting defensive battles (and are usually defeated), the proletarians of the emerging countries are waging militant reformist struggles, and are often successful, with hardly any convergence between the two. Besides, though the deepening of the crisis leads to multi-fold reactions to unemployment and impoverishment and a sharpening of class unrest, nothing shows that this radicalisation is taking a communist turn. There is always more than one single way out of a major crisis. Let's remember the 1930s . . . We live epochal times: an epoch includes setbacks as well as advances.

[2] Nevertheless, as a future communist revolution would be an unprecedented phenomenon, its warning signs might well be indecipherable, even to the most farsighted, so we cannot neglect the possibility that some more or less near future would come to us as a positive surprise.

A quantum of solace: forecasters are usually wrong, radical ones no exception. In January 1917, Lenin declared: "We older men perhaps will not live to see the coming revolution." A few weeks later, revolution broke out in Petrograd.

5) The Proletariat as a Contradiction

One last quote by Marx: "I do not claim to have discovered either the existence of classes in modern society or the struggle between them."[7] It is no use endlessly proving the permanence of a confrontation that is plain to see. Our concern is that it could *end*, by a communist revolution that has to arise in a society shaped and torn by the interaction of proletarians and bourgeois. Our "problem" is how class struggle will be able to produce something else than its own continuation.

Is there a contradiction here, and a major one?

Yes. But the sole question is whether this contradiction cannot be solved . . . or can be.

Up to now, most of the time, even in a combative way, proletarians have fought to improve their lot within this society: labour tries to get the most out of capital, not to abolish the labour/capital couple. Acknowledging this is a primary condition to understand what the communist movement has to face.

The proletarians are placed at the same time *inside* and *outside* capitalism, and act accordingly. They straddle two worlds: they are *in* this world and not *of* this world. The bourgeois live, prosper, and stay inside a social logic which is beneficial to them. Only the proletarians have the potential leverage to transform the present order of things . . .

Which does not mean that they will. Resisting oppression and exploitation is not the same as doing away with oppression and exploitation altogether. We are not dismissive about what is called cash-and-hours agenda: we just say such demands fail to bring the proletarians together. Convergence will only take place against wage-labour and the society based upon it.

There are better dreams.

■ NOTES

Preface to the Japanese Edition

1   *Le Mouvement Communiste* was a bulletin published in France, 1972–74. There was also a book with the same title (1972). An extract, "Capital and State," can be read in English on the For Communism–John Gray site, http://www.reocities.com/~johngray/capstat.htm.

2   Paul Mattick, "Otto Rühle and the German Labour Movement," 1945, https://www.marxists.org/archive/mattick-paul/1945/otto-ruhle.htm.

3   Academia is not what it used to be. As a prominent production place of established knowledge, the university has kept its prestige, but lost its privilege when it merged with business and media. *Acamedia* would be a better word. Because it is a reflection of society, the university differs in 2013 from 1913 or even 1953. Marx was rarely taught in most Western countries until after World War II, the (less and less Marxist, actually) "Frankfurt School" in the United States being an exception. It all changed in the 1960s, for better (lecturers discussing Marx's concept of alienation), or worse (comparing the merits of Mao with those of Althusser). After the 1970s, with the demise of the western worker movement, public *class* discourse became outmoded. A global universal shapeless critique now prevails, where Debord meets Spinoza and Deleuze, alongside radical geography, unorthodox economics, peace studies, environment studies, gender studies, post-colonial studies . . . A century ago, Arthur Cravan said there would come a day when everyone in the street would be an artist. We are all critics now. Capitalist democracy excels in self-examination.

4   Though it may look odd to qualify the 1920s–30s as "counter-revolutionary," the fact is that after the post-1917 earthquake, revolution suffered one defeat after another, in different contrasted forms: bureaucratic dictatorship in Russia, fascism in Italy, powerful social-democrat and Stalinist parties in the West, authoritarian regimes in Eastern Europe, and Nazism to cap it all. In 1936, the Spanish revolutionary wave—one of the highest points ever reached by proletarian action—occurred in such a negative context that the insurgents were ultimately doomed.

5   In the 1970s, the official left consisted of social-democrat and Stalinist parties. The CPs were still quite strong in France, Italy, Spain, Portugal, and several Latin American countries like Argentina or Chile, and supported by a predominantly militant yet reformist working class, so these parties were able to blunt the edge of class struggle.

By "pseudo-revolutionary groups," we meant Maoists and Trotskyists.

Now the picture has changed. Hardly any comment is needed on the decline of Western CPs. The CPUSA and the CPBG have self-euthanised. There is not much left of the Italian CP, and the French one only retains some power in local government and the CGT union federation. The far left has been unable to fill the vacuum, in spite of its constant effort to appear less radical and more acceptable: revolutionary pretence is over, and social ambitions have been downsized to a "Share the riches" programme, of course with an ecological touch. This does not mean that political forces like the German *Linke*, the French Left Front (which the much declined CP is part of, and where its members meet up with ex-Trots) or the Greek Syriza have lost *all* political significance. Though "frontlines" have shifted and demarcations are blurred, the left and far left retain a capacity to contain and stifle many an autonomous movement.

6   Advocating a "return to Marx" is as imperative now as it used to be, providing Marx himself is addressed too. See chapter 5: "Value, Time, and Communism: Re-reading Marx."

7   Today I would not write that the IS had no "understanding of capital." While its critique focused more on commodity than on capital, on alienation than on exploitation, it did not ignore the wage-labour/capital relation, hence class struggle, though Situationists approached it via an emphasis on commodity.

Foreword to the 1974 Black & Red Edition

1   "Militant" is positive in English: it denotes true commitment and eagerness to fight. The French meaning is closer to Latin etymology: the term was borrowed from army vocabulary: the militant acts like a political *soldier*. See the now-classic "Militancy: The Highest Stage of Alienation," by the French group OJTR, 1972, available at https://libcom.org/library/militancy-ojtr.

2   On the one hand, "security" has become a boom industry. On the other, police in the streets now often look and sometimes act like soldiers.

3   See above preface, n.5.

4   Ken Weller, *1970–72: The Lordstown Struggle and the Real Crisis in Production*, Solidarity Pamphlet, 1973. Contrary to what we believed at the time, "the union controlled the anger of the worker." See "In

the Heart of the Heart of the Country: The Strike at Lordstown," available at http://www.prole.info/texts/heartofheart.html.

5   The U.S. Students for a Democratic Society disbanded in 1969, the German SDS in 1970. They had been born out of student rebellion against nuclear armaments, the Vietnam War, racism, masculine domination, consumerism, authority, etc. Both were broad organisations covering a wide range of issues and involving a large number of participants with frequently conflicting views.

6   Ernest Mandel (1923–95): one of the leaders of the Trotskyist Fourth International and its main economist: see the critical review of his *Marxist Economic Theory* (1968, 2 vols.) by Paul Mattick, *Mandel's Economics* (1969), https://www.marxists.org/archive/mattick-paul/1969/mandel.htm. Paul Sweezy (1910–2004), academic Marxist, specialist of monopoly capitalism, Harry Magdoff (1913–2006), anti-imperialist and Third-Worldist socialist. Like Sweezy, one of the editors of *The Monthly Review*. These writers are not widely read anymore, and their place has been taken by an array of similar critics who describe what's wrong with this world without knowing why. They want wage-labour to be fair and money to be invested in the "real economy." They are aware that big business runs democracy, and would like it the other way round. They have one thing in common: they are *economists*. Communist theory is a critique of the economy: this is a marker delineating the parting of the ways. Today's soft left is as anti-revolutionary as hard Stalinists used to be.

7   *Ceylon: The JVP Uprising of April 1971* (London: Solidarity, 1972), available at https://libcom.org/history/ceylon-jvp-uprising-april-1971.

Foreworld: Out of the Future

1   The French documentary *Reprise*, by Hervé Le Roux, was released in 1996.

2   Shams al-Din Hafez, fourteenth century.

3   "Captive Words," in *Situationist International* no. 10, 1966.

4   Paul Virilio has invented *dromology*, the science and logic of speed (*Speed and Politics*, 1977). In true postmodernist fashion, he is quite good at sometimes brilliant descriptions of social phenomena the structure and cause of which he does not perceive, nor is really interested in.

5   Andrew Miles and Mike Savage, *The Remaking of the British Working Class, 1840–1940* (New York: Routledge, 1994).

6   When social ties come unloose and no human community is yet emerging, closed-in communities spring up. The swelling tide of nationalist, regionalist, ethno-religious, xenophobic grouplets and parties since the 1990s is not to be minimised, nor their ability to exploit ethnic fault lines and pit one group against another. In

future turbulent times, they will complement the official repression agencies in breaking strikes, disrupting meetings, beating up radicals, planting bombs, etc. However, this is different from interwar fascism. Mussolini and Hitler smashed a worker movement which the bourgeoisie perceived as a threat (a bit rightly, mostly mistakenly, but after all the Russian revolution did wipe out the bourgeois ruling class, before installing a new kind of—bureaucratic—capitalist class). Today's far right is a marginal anti-revolutionary force compared to police and army, whether they get their orders from a right-wing or a left-wing government. So far.

7   Paolo Spriano, *The Occupation of the Italian Factories: Italy 1920* (London: Pluto Press, 1975), available at https://libcom.org/history/occupation-factories-italy-1920-paolo-spriano.

8   In 2009, the French Trotskyist Ligue Communiste Révolutionnaire became the Nouveau Parti Anti-Capitaliste. If language means anything, giving up the *revolution* denotation was significant, as was trading a reference to a positive programmatic content for a general statement of opposition to capitalism.

9   In the early 1980s, supposedly docile South Korean labour grew into an insubordinate social force. A few landmarks: the 1980 Gwangju popular rising crushed by the army; the 1987 "Great Labour Struggle"; the 1996–97 general strike.

   On Albania in 1997, see "Upheaval in the Land of the Eagles" (TPTG, 1998), available at https://libcom.org/library/upheaval-land-eagles.

Chapter 1: Capitalism and Communism

1   Marshall Sahlins, "The Original Affluent Society," in *Stone Age Economics* (Chicago: Aldine, 1972).

2   Gregory Clark, *A Farewell to Alms: A Brief Economic History of the World* (Princeton University Press, 2008).

3   Fredy Perlman, *The Reproduction of Daily Life* (Detroit: Black & Red, 1969).

4   Paul Kennedy, *The Rise and Fall of the Great Powers: Economic Change and Military Powers 1500–2000* (New York: Random House, 1987); Immanuel Wallerstein, *Historical Capitalism* (London: Verso, 1983); Giovanni Arrighi and Beverly Silver, *Chaos and Governance in the Modern World System* (Minneapolis: University of Minnesota Press, 1999).

5   Sorry for the old-fashioned cliché. Today's bourgeoisie has been updated and even increasingly *genderised*: a woman became head of the IMF in 2011, another is currently Facebook's COO, etc.

6   Marx, *Poverty of Philosophy*, 1847, chap. 1, section 2.

7   On value formation and *de*-formation in the USSR, see *Aufheben* no. 9, 2000.

8   Though there are exceptions, most of those companies called *multi-national* are first and foremost U.S., Japanese, Chinese, etc. The theory of a world company, an international ruling financial oligarchy, or a post-nation-State *empire* (as in Negri and Hardt's 2000 bestseller), is not documented by facts. As demonstrated by the pre-1914 economic internationalisation, closer interconnections on the world market go together with competing monopolies and antagonistic political entities or blocs. In the twenty-first century, national States are still warring with one another economically . . . for the moment. The bourgeoisie may be cosmopolitan, and capital indeed flows worldwide online every second, but the planet remains divided between contending political entities, large or small, with the oddity of an economic giant that remains politically feeble: Europe.

9   In the 1946–47 famine in Russia, estimates vary from one to two million deaths. At the end of the 1950s, millions starved in China. In both cases, climatic factors and government policy coalesced to create chaos and catastrophe.

10 Since we wrote the first version of "Capitalism and Communism" in 1972, "anti-industrialism" has come to the fore. The anti-industrial critique points to an essential feature of capitalism, but mistakes the part for the whole. Industry is certainly *at the centre* of the present world and it is hard to imagine a non-industrial capitalism. The "post-industrial society" is a myth now as it was in 1970. Yet industry is not *the centre* of capitalism. We are not faced with a self-propelled freewheeling mega-machine, but with a value-driven productive system. The techno-bureaucratic-industrial monster has to abide by the constraints of labour productivity and capital profitability. Big business only wants larger factories and more machines if they bring in more value: otherwise, it leaves them to rot, moves elsewhere, speculates, or stays idle. Capitalist history is as much industrial wasteland (the U.S. rust belt, or the empty European factories zoned for reclamation) as formidable mega-machinery.

11 *The American Worker*, 1947, chap. 2, http://www.prole.info/pdfs/americanworker.pdf.

12 This passage has been left nearly as it was written in 1973. It might make strange reading after a few decades of growth and crisis, but is the world picture immensely different in 2013 from the one we painted forty years ago? As before, capitalism's Promethean progress is paralleled with an equally innovative catastrophic power. Life expectancy has gone up, yet nearly one billion people go hungry every day, and it's easier for the Indian poor to use a cell phone than have access to clean water.

    However, we will not look for vindication in the "worst" aspects of this world (dire misery, over-exploitation of Asian or Latin

American labour, etc.). Capitalism's supporters have their twofold answer ready: "These people's lot used to be worse, and soon it'll get better." (Curiously, this is what the defenders of Stalinist Russia used to say.) Therefore we will not focus on the most visible forms of poverty in "rich" countries, like what Michael. Harrington wrote on *The Other America* in 1962. Our indictment will not deal with environmental issues either, however serious they are: there's enough ecological talk going round for everyone to see capitalism's waste propensity. We'd rather take a look at the supposedly "best" or "good" aspects of contemporary society.

Let's not consider what capitalism denies or destroys, but what it offers. It prides itself on giving us rewarding jobs: for once, let us judge a system in accordance with its own values. Here are the top ten jobs that most people do in the United States, according to the official Bureau of Labor Statistics (2010): 1) retail salespeople, 2) cashiers, 3) office clerks, 4) combined food preparation and serving workers (fast food workers), 5) registered nurses, 6) waiters and waitresses, 7) customer service representatives (mostly telemarketing), 8) manual freight and stock movers (as opposed to people who move things with forklifts), 9) janitors and cleaners (not including maids), 10) stock clerks and order fillers. Apart from nurses, this list does not only mean low pay, job insecurity, and lack of recognition, but monotony, techno-slaving, physical discomfort, and low "human" content of the labour performed. Besides, reformers deplore the "evil" world of marketing and advertising, but fail to realise the parasitic nature of the ever-growing armies of psychosocial specialists (alleviators of social ills, mediators, trainers, coaches, facilitators, etc.), of communicators, of researchers, of media workers . . . and of security personnel (one million in the United States). A society where a "correction industry" employs more people than Ford, GM, and Walmart combined does not merely "waste" natural resources: human ones as well.

Moreover, "Nobody in the 1950s or 1960s could have guessed that the average Americans in 2000 would be working longer hours or that their incomes, in real, inflation-adjusted terms, would not have risen in a generation." (Michael Lind, *Land of Promise*, New York: Harper, 2012), chap. 16.

We'll let the naïve delude themselves with the belief that sensible, eco-friendly Denmark does far better than outrageous, cruel America. It may well be, but a century of Scandinavian social-democracy has proved unable to uproot poverty: local reformers only pride themselves on getting rid of *extreme* poverty. Capitalism remains a grinding system: "The organisation of the workers and their constantly growing resistance will possibly stem the *growth of misery* to a certain extent. But the *insecurity of existence* will surely grow." (Engels, *Critique of the Erfurt Programme*, 1891).

13 Brazil's last decades of growth seem to contradict this bleak picture, especially since ex-metal worker Lula was elected president in 2003, and promised to put an end to "social apartheid": thanks to agro-business and local manufacturing for multinationals, wealth would "trickle down" to the poor. More modestly, his successor at the head of the "world's seventh economy" has merely claimed to have done away with *dire* misery. So much for ending social apartheid. In 1844, the future Napoleon III published *The Extinction of Pauperism*. No emperor, no union leader turned statesman can get rid of the dispossession which lies at the root of—and is reproduced by—capitalism.

14 The concept of "those who have no reserves" was formulated by Amadeo Bordiga in the years following World War II. Bordiga's purpose was not to create a new definition of the proletariat, but to go back to the general definition. Marx's *Capital* can only be understood when read with earlier analyses of the proletariat, for instance *The Economic and Philosophic Manuscripts of 1844*, the *Contribution to the Critique of Hegel's Philosophy of Right: Introduction*, 1843, and the 1857–58 manuscripts, often referred to by their German title: *The Grundrisse*.

15 *A Contribution to the Critique of Hegel's Philosophy of Right: Introduction*, 1843.

16 *Communist Manifesto*, chap. I

17 *Le Communisme—tentative de définition*, part IV (1998): www.hicsalta-communisation.com. Also by Bruno Astarian, *Crisis Activity and Communisation*, 2011, http://libcom.org/library/crisis-activity-communisation-bruno-astarian.

18 Marx's letter to Vera Zasulich, first draft, April 1881. The whole draft deserves to be read.

19 Since the 1970s, modern democratic advanced societies have become a lot more flexible in accepting alternativist social experiments. There are more and more examples of passive housing and eco-building. On the Vauban "sustainable model district" in Freiburg (Germany), see *Green Gone Wrong: The Broken Promise of the Eco-Friendly Economy* (London: Verso, 2010), chap. 3, by Heather Rogers (by no means an anti-ecologist). A thorough investigation.

20 Engels, *Conditions and Prospects of a War of the Holy Alliance against a Revolutionary France in 1852*, 1851.

21 Dauvé and Denis Authier, *The Communist Left in Germany, 1918–21*, available at https://libcom.org/library/communist-left-germany-1918-1921; on Spain 1936–39, Dauvé, *When Insurrections Die*, available at http://www.troploin.fr/node/47.

22 Situationist International, "The Decline and Fall of the Spectacle Commodity Economy," *Situationist International* no. 10, 1966.

23 Since 1973, the ex-Third World and the ex-"socialist bloc" have given birth to several "emerging countries." We do not equate industrialisation with communist potentials. However, a social system first reaches its breaking point where its fundamental contradictions (capital/labour, in the case of capitalism) are the sharpest and can have the most explosive impact. Though class struggle erupts everywhere, communist revolution is more likely to be *initiated* in the United States than in the Congo, and in China more in Shanghai than in Karakorum. After this, Congolese and Mongolese proletarians will contribute as much as those from the United States and from Chinese metropolises.

24 Of course workers "as they are now" have managing capabilities, as proved by the continual creation of cooperatives. Myriads of co-ops have appeared in the last decades (Portugal after 1974, Towers Colliery in Wales, Argentina in 2001 . . .) and many more spring up every year. We do not deny that they often help people get jobs, self-help, community services, and sometimes function on the principles of equal pay and decision-sharing. Still, they make up for the deficiencies of capital and State, and a million co-ops will never will be a threat to Big Business . . . except for a few successful co-ops lucky or unlucky enough to become Big Business themselves. Likewise, *micro-credit* is finance adapted to the poor (not the *very* poor).

25 Especially in *The King of Prussia and Social Reform*, also in *The Jewish Question*, and in his analysis of Jacobinism as the paroxysm of the political over the social spirit. In the 1840s, Marx immersed himself extensively in the French Revolution, and many of his notes and comments can be now read as an implicit but direct critique of Bolshevik policy after 1917.

26 Engels, "Progress of Social Reform on the Continent," *The New Moral World*, April 4, 1843. Decades later, he suggested "that *Gemeinwesen* ["commonalty" or collective being] be universally substituted for *state*; it is a good old German word that can very well do service for the French *Commune*" (letter to A. Bebel, March 18–28, 1875).

27 For more on democracy, see our "A Contribution to the Critique of Political Autonomy," 2008, http://www.troploin.fr/node/17.

Chapter 2: The Class Struggle and Its Most Characteristic Aspects in Recent Years

1 If the Censier-based committee had cared to publicise its action, it might have made a name for itself and would now be as famous as the Situationist-influenced CMDO, the Council for the Maintenance of Occupations. The CMDO, described by the SI as "a link, not a power," was active in the Sorbonne from May 10 to 15, when it

decided to break up and its participants moved to another university building, ten minutes' walk from both the Sorbonne and Censier.

In the situationist history of '68, *Enragés & Situationists in the Occupations Movement*, (1968, English translation by Autonomedia, 1992) René Viénet writes disparagingly about Censier: "Other 'councilist' tendencies (in the sense that they were for the councils without wanting to recognize their theory and their truth) appeared in the buildings of the Censier annex of the Faculté des Lettres, where they held, as the "Worker-Student Action Committee," a somewhat impotent discussion which could hardly progress towards a practical clarification. Groups like "Workers' Power" and the "Workers' Liaison and Action Group," made up of many individuals from various enterprises, made the mistake of accepting into their already confused and redundant debates all kinds of adversaries or saboteurs of their positions—Trotskyists and Maoists who paralyzed the discussion, and who even publicly burned an anti-bureaucratic program drawn up by a commission assigned to the task. The councilists were able to intervene in some practical struggles, notably at the beginning of the general strike, by sending members to help in a work stoppage or to reinforce picket lines. But their interventions often suffered from defects inherent in their very grouping: often several members from a single delegation offered fundamentally conflicting perspectives to the workers."

Viénet is as self-satisfied about the CMDO (hence, the SI and himself) as dismissive of Censier. He conflates the undeniable deficiencies of councilism with what the Censier Action Committees really did. Ironically, the Situationists owed a lot more to councilism than they ever realised, and a large part of the critique of ultra-leftist ideology developed in the next text would apply to the SI: see chap. 4, note 1. The CMDO certainly had posters and leaflets widely circulated, in France and abroad, whereas Censier was a lot more connected to workplaces, but the truth is, both were among the best radical aspects of '68.

On our critique of the SI: *Critique of the SI* (1979); *Back to the SI* (2000), available at http://www.troploin.fr/node/5; *The SI*, extract from *The Story of Our Origins*, *La Banquise* #2, 1983. All available on the johngray site. Also *And the SI?*, from *La Banquise* no. 4, 1986, available at http://thesinisterquarter.wordpress.com/2013/06/08/and-the-s-i/.

For an active participants' view of Censier: Fredy Perlman, R. Gregoire: *Worker-Student Action Committees: France, May '68* (Detroit: Black & Red, 1969), and Lorraine Perlman's biography *Having Little, Being Much: A Chronicle of Fredy Perlman's Fifty Years* (Detroit: Black & Red, 1989), available on the Anarchist Library site.

2 Gierek was the Polish party leader and ruler of the country from 1970 to 1980.

3   In 1983, the French socialist government granted labour the right
     to a full pension at 60 (on the condition of a 37.5 year contribution).
     Needless to say, since then, things have repeatedly changed for the
     worst, under left and right governments.

4   This was true of Poland in the early and mid-1970s. Whereas in
     democratic countries, only a minority of the labour force rejected
     the unions, in bureaucratic regimes, the mass of workers dis-
     trusted unions which were part of the State apparatus. But when
     Solidarnosc was born in 1980 as a grassroots militant union, it had
     a large genuine working class support. Solidarnosc combined social
     and national-democratic demands, which was to be expected in
     the context of a popular revolt against a dictatorial regime backed
     and controlled by a foreign power (the USSR). With the benefit of
     hindsight, it is now easy to realise that the 1970s Polish worker
     resistance and rebellion were not part of an ascending communist
     movement. Solidarnosc eventually became legal, helped form the
     first post-bureaucratic government, and its leader and symbol, Lech
     Walesa, was elected President of the Republic.

5   After 1972 in France, and in the late '70s in Italy, the revolutionary
     tide that François Martin and the rest of us expected to rise started
     to fall. Since then, unionism has gone downhill, without fading away
     completely. While in the West and Japan, blue collar unionisation
     in the manufacturing and mining sectors has considerably declined,
     union density has sometimes increased in the service and public
     sector, particularly in the United States. In Asian, Latin American,
     and South African factories, unions can be very active, and new ones
     are born. As long as capitalism exists, as long as labour confronts
     capital, labour will resist and organise one way or another.

6   This 1972 statement may sound odd forty years later, still we hold
     it to be valid. Growing unemployment in the West goes together
     with a global increase in the number of wage earners, not only in
     the United States but also in France, and even more so on a world
     scale, where millions of people have been forced into the hardship of
     modern labour in the last decades, all over Asia in particular. As for
     France, although the proportion of "manual workers" has decreased
     in relation to the whole working population, in absolute figures
     they are more numerous than they were in 1972. We do not live in a
     post-industrial society.

7   Two writings by Émile Pouget (1860–1931) can be read under
     the title "Sabotage," a short 1898 text (https://www.marxists.
     org/archive/pouget/1898/sabotage.htm) and a 1912 book (http://
     theanarchistlibrary.org/library/emile-pouget-sabotage).

8   "Job enrichment" was to prove more ideological than real. In the
     1970s, in the old industrial metropolises, bosses failed to promote

worker participation in the running of the shop floor. Since then, ruthless neo-Taylorism in the "New Industrialized Countries" has made a sham of worker participation. Instead of motivating labour by giving it minor responsibilities, business operates on the "Do as you're told" principle. Whatever "job enrichment" there is takes the form of compulsory multi-tasking.

9 The Parti Socialiste Unifié (PSU) was an odd mixture of people disillusioned by the old official socialist party (called SFIO, which was in office many times after 1945, supported colonial wars, repressed strikes, etc.), and of younger elements in search for a militant modern social democracy. At the same time, a prominent PSU member, Pierre Mendès-France, was a long-time politician, ex-minister and even head of state in 1954–55. Unlike the "workerist" CP, the PSU stood for a "new working class" where technicians and white collar employees would be able to take part in managing the firm. Various PSU members became famous among the spokespersons of May 1968, and later influential in the CFDT. Some leaders later joined the new Socialist Party (PS). After several splits, the PSU disbanded in 1990.

The Confédération Française Démocratique du Travail was born in 1919 as the CFTC (second "C" for *Christian*): an anti-CGT, anti-socialist union, until it gave up the religious reference in 1966 and became the CFDT, a more open, more "democratic," more tolerant federation than the CGT. Though it organised far less factory workers than its rival, it had a few local strongholds in industry. After 1968, the CFDT developed a pro-self-management discourse which attracted a number of young militant workers and was in tune with the spirit of the time. A decade later, social utopian well-wishing paled before hard economic reality: the CFDT's demands and policy became even more "class accommodationist" than those of the CP-controlled CGT.

Both PSU and CFDT stood at the crossroads of the old declining "worker movement" and a rising modernist broader "social movement." Both had their heyday in 1973–74 when the LIP watch-making plant was occupied and partly self-managed by the labour force. For a while, LIP was a symbol of fraternal worker mutual creativity, as opposed to bureaucratic undemocratic statist socialism favoured by the CGT and CP.

10 The French CP's general secretary made it perfectly clear in 1970: "There are workers we'll never defend: those who smash machines or cars they manufacture."

11 The merger failed to materialise: in 2013, UIL, CISL, and CGIL still exist as three separate union federations.

12 Like the SI roughly at the same time, this text regarded Italy as a research lab of proletarian action and capitalist counter-offensive. In the 1970s, Italy was to display a rich variety of workers' autonomy:

indiscipline, absenteeism, meetings on the shop floor without notice, demos on the premises to call for a strike, wildcat picketing, block-ade of goods . . . A permanent feature was the rejection of hierarchy: equal pay rise, no privileged category, free speech . . . Another aspect was the attempt to go beyond the distinction between representa-tion and action in the functioning of the rank-and-file committees. Such self-organisation was essential as a means of collective action, but when it failed as an organ of a social change that did not come about, it disappeared with the rest of the proletarian surge.

It was no accident that the big factory committees of northern Italy were only loosely connected: resisting the boss can be a local matter, whereas reorganising production and social life means going out of one's workplace.

Chapter 3: A Crash Course in Ultra-Leftology

1   For a good start, Philippe Bourrinet's in-depth historical studies: *The Italian Communist Left*; *The Bordigist Current 1919–1999: Italy, France, Belgium*; and *The German-Dutch Communist Left*, all on left-dis.nl.

Gilles Dauvé and Denis Authier, *The Communist Left in Germany, 1918–21*, English translation available on libcom, https://libcom.org/library/communist-left-germany-1918-1921.

Two extracts from *The Story of Our Origins*, published in *La Banquise* no. 2, 1983: "From the German Left to Socialisme ou Barbarie," and "The Italian Left & Bordiga," on the johngray site.

As there is a dark legend on Bordiga during the fascist era, to get the record straight, we recommend "An Important Book on Bordiga Unknown 1926–46," available at http://www.left-dis.nl/uk/bordigaunknowm.htm.

Philippe Bourrinet's very informative studies do not deal much with the theoretical work of the "late" Bordiga: see Bordiga's *Murdering the Dead: Amadeo Bordiga on Capitalism and Other Disasters* (London: Antagonism, 2001). Unfortunately, most of Bordiga can only be read in Italian and French.

Chapter 4: Leninism and the Ultra-Left

1   Historians of the SI and Debord's biographers tend to play down the influence Socialisme ou Barbarie exerted on the SI. What SoB as a group really tried, did, and became is obscured by the celeb-rity of its "animating personality," Cornelius Castoriadis. For a good short account: Marcel van der Linden, *Socialisme ou Barbarie, A French Revolutionary Group (1949–65)*, 1997, http://www.left-dis.nl/uk/lindsob.htm. (Regrettably, van den Linden does not mention the SI-SoB connection.) Anselm Jappe's good biography, *Guy Debord* (Berkeley: University of California Press, 1999), says little on Debord's passage

in the SoB group. To the best of our knowledge, the only English language articles that deal substantially with this relation are by Bill Brown, on the notbored.org site.

This is not the time for an essay on the SI, but the situationist vision differed greatly from the usual councilist approach. If daily life is given its real broad sense, extending *worker* management to generalised *self*-management of daily life meant a qualitative leap which exploded the concept of work and managing . . . and therefore of workers' councils: if you modify the whole of life, then production, workplace, work, and the economy cannot exist as separate domains anymore.

The SI indirectly addressed councilism when it criticised "a one-sided, undialectical, and insufficiently historical manner by some of the radical groups who are halfway between the old degraded and mystified conception of the workers movement, which they have superseded, and the new form of total contestation which is yet to come. (See, for example, the significant theories of Cardan and others in the journal *Socialisme ou Barbarie*.)" For the SI, "the very core of the revolutionary project . . . is nothing less than the suppression of work in the usual present-day sense (and of the proletariat) and of all the justifications of previous forms of work." ("Ideologies, Classes and the Domination of Nature," *Situationist International* no. 8 (1963): see Situationist International Online). The reference is probably to *On the Content of Socialism*, by Cardan-Castoriadis, published in *S ou B* in 1955, available at http://eagainst.com/articles/castor/.

2   Our *Notes pour une analyse de la Révolution russe* was later integrated in the book *Communisme & Question russe*, still available in the Editions Spartacus catalogue, yet never translated into English. Two years later, the English group Solidarity (which had been close to SoB) published *The Bolsheviks and Workers' Control: The State and Counter-revolution*, by Maurice Brinton, who wrote in the introduction: "That such an analysis might be possible was suggested in an excellent short pamphlet *Notes pour une analyse . . .*" The interpretative framework of worker v. bureaucratic power could only please the theorists of worker management.

3   ICO later became and is still active as Echanges & Mouvement: mondialisme.org.

4   *Reading ICO*, *SI* no. 11, 1967; also *What Makes ICO Lie?*, no. 12, 1969. For ICO/Echanges & Mouvement's point of view: *ICO & l'IS: Retour sur les relations entre ICO et l'IS*, 2007 (mondialisme.org; as far as we know, it has not been translated into English).

5   At the same time (1969) as our informal group was writing this critique of councilism, we published *The "Renegade" Lenin & His Disciple Kautsky*, now in English on the John Gray site.

6   Marx's letter to Ferdinand Freiligrath, February 29, 1860. "Marx and Engels derived the characteristics of the party form from the description of communist society." (Jacques Camatte, "Origin and Function of the Party Form," 1961, available in English https://www.marxists.org/archive/camatte/origin.htm). An illuminating comment.

7   Lenin, *On the Duality of Power*, April 9, 1917; Marx, *German Ideology*, Part I, D, 1845–46. For more on power, see chap. 1, section 12 in this volume.

8   Council communists would reply that the workers' management they envisage is entirely different from capitalism. As we will argue in the next chapter, their scheme maintains the fundamentals of capitalism, because it is based on labour time counting.

9   On Spain: Gilles Dauvé, *When Insurrections Die*, 1998, http://www.troploin.fr/node/47.

Chapter 5: Value, Time, and Communism: Re-reading Marx

1   Several essential points made in this chapter derive from Bruno Astarian's stimulating *Feuilleton* (serial) on value, chapters 1 and 2 (on the Hic Salta site, so far only in French).

2   Rosa Luxemburg, *Stagnation and Progress of Marxism*, 1903, https://www.marxists.org/archive/luxemburg/1903/misc/stagnation.htm.

3   Preface to *A Contribution to the Critique of Political Economy*, 1859.

4   All *Grundrisse* quotes are taken from Notebook VII, "Contradiction between the foundation of bourgeois production (value as measure) and its development. Machines, etc."

5   *Fundamental Principles of Communist Production & Distribution*, GIK, 1930, Epilogue, section 2: "From Money to Labour-Time Computation."

6   German-born Jan Appel (1890–1985) was active in the KAPD, then had to move to Holland where he joined the Dutch council communist group GIK. His 1966 short autobiography is readable on libcom.

7   *Un monde sans argent: le communisme*, published in France in 1975–76 by the OJTR group. Available in English at https://libcom.org/library/world-without-money-communism-les-amis-de-4-millions-de-jeunes-travailleurs.

8   *The Content of Socialism/Communism*, by D.G., 1994 (http://www.left-dis.nl/uk/consoc.htm). If the GIK and Mattick could have read the then-unpublished *Grundrisse* in the 1930s, it is likely that Marx's pages would have fuelled their thesis rather than thrown cold water on it. When they consider the *Grundrisse*, contemporary councilists like D.G. find confirmation in Marx's passages on time.

9   Paul Mattick, *What Is Communism?*, *International Council Correspondence* 1 (October 1934): https://bataillesocialiste.wordpress.com/english-pages/1934-10-what-is-communism-mattick.

10   In 1932, under the name of Carl Steuermann, Rühle published a book (available in French, not in English) the title of which translates as: "World Crisis; or, Towards State Capitalism."

Although his 1939 book (first published in French) remained in obscurity for thirty years, Bruno Rizzi (1901–77) was one of the first to theorise the *Bureaucratization of the World*.

In 1939–40, in the American Trotskyist SWP, James Burnham and Max Schachtman rejected Trotsky's thesis of the USSR as a "degenerated workers' State," and demonstrated that the bureaucracy was an exploiting class and the Russian State imperialist. Burnham soon turned arch-conservative and became a dedicated Cold Warrior. Schachtman evolved towards a more and more moderate social democracy.

Adolf Berle and Gardiner Means were among those who promoted the theory of corporate governance (*The Modern Corporation and Private Property*, 1932). Berle was involved in the New Deal.

Joseph Schumpeter's influential book was *Capitalism, Socialism, and Democracy* (New York: Harper, 1942).

11   Karl Korsch, "Ten Theses on Marxism Today," 1950, available at https://www.marxists.org/archive/korsch/1950/ten-theses.htm.

12   Needless to say, Bordiga's cogent objections were left unanswered, partly because they came from a staunch defender of Lenin.

In his Marxist days, Castoriadis (then writing as Pierre Chaulieu) regarded value as a mere instrument of measure, a useful concept, not as the *reality* of capital. In *Marx and Keynes* (1969), Mattick interpreted the analysis of value as a critique of the superficial nature of classical economics: he did not see it as a social mechanism characteristic of capitalism.

One more word on value. In "Marx's Critique of Socialist Labor-Money Schemes and the Myth of Council Communism's Proudhonism," (available at libcom), David Adam rebuts my former critique of the councilist vision of communism on the ground that the GIK's notion of value is the same as Marx's. The discussion is becoming rather tricky, no fault of Adam's or mine, it is just that the question is complicated. In the previous editions of "Leninism and the Ultra-Left," I wished to refute the GIK in the name of Marx's analysis of value, with reference to the *Grundrisse* especially. This 2013 chapter now makes the point that there is something highly debatable in Marx's vision itself, both in *Capital* and the *Grundrisse*, and that the GIK *did* follow Marx's footsteps and was wrong to do so: far from being a useful and fair instrument of measure, labour time is capitalist blood. This is more than a causative link: labour time *is* the substance of value. Marx was indeed a forerunner of the councilist project. Let it be clear, however, that our present critique of Marx is also possible because of what we read in his writings.

13 Oddly enough first published in Moscow in the maelstrom of World War II, the *Grundrisse* remained virtually unknown until the second German edition (1953), it was made available in French only in 1967, and English readers had to wait until 1973 for a full translation.

14 Antonio Negri, *Marx beyond Marx: Lessons on the Grundrisse* (Brooklyn: Autonomedia, 1991). "Value form" theorists like Robert Kurz are equally wrong to believe that capitalism by its own contemporary evolution would be dissolving the substance of abstract labour that is the productive basis of capital.

15 On Marx and the Russian *mir*, see his letter to Vera Zasulich, March 8, 1881: a quote from the first draft is in our chapter 1, section 10 on communisation; and: "If the Russian Revolution becomes the signal for a proletarian revolution in the West, so that both complement each other, the present Russian common ownership of land may serve as the starting point for a communist development," (preface to the 1882 edition of the *Communist Manifesto*); also Engels's prescient remarks in his letter to Zasulich, April 23, 1885.

16 *Speech on the Question of Free Trade*, January 1848.

Chapter 6: The Bitter Victory of Councilism

1 In part 3 of *The Life and Death of Democracy* (New York: Pocket Books, 2010), John Keane is a stalwart defender of monitory democracy. Otherwise, a well-documented and worth reading history book.

Chapter 7: Postlude

1 For more on that period and our background, see *The Story of Our Origins* (translated from *La Banquise*, 1983), www.reocities.com/~johngray. And our *What's It All About?*, 2007, http://www.troploin.fr/node/48.

2 Marx & Engels, *Fictitious Splits in the International*, 1872.

3 See above, chap. 5, sections 7 and 8.

4 Herman Gorter, *Open Letter to Comrade Lenin*, 1920, conclusion, https://www.marxists.org/archive/gorter/1920/open-letter/.

5 Eric Hobsbawm, *The Machine Breakers*, 1952, http://libcom.org/history/machine-breakers-eric-hobsbawm.

6 In the 1930s, some revolutionaries mistook the ascent of rank-and-file militancy with the emergence of an altogether different working class (Canne Meijer, *The Rise of a New Labour Movement*, 1938). The proletarian surge later gave birth to the CIO's industrial unionism, which complemented the old AFL craft unions ill-adapted to modern industry. History surely does not repeat itself, but . . .

7 Marx's letter to J. Weydemeyer, March 5, 1852, https://www.marxists.org/archive/marx/works/1852/letters/52_03_05-ab.htm.

■ ABOUT THE AUTHORS

Born in 1947, **Gilles Dauvé** has worked as a translator and a schoolteacher. He is the author of essays and books on the Russian, German, and Spanish revolutions, and on democracy, fascism, war, morals, crisis, and class. Most infamously, in English, his texts *What Is Situationism?* and *Fascism/Anti-Fascism* (both written under the pseudonym Jean Barrot) have led a legendary existence in the samizdat pamphlet underground. Many of his writings can be read at http://www.troploin.fr.

Born in Algeria in a family of European settlers in 1941, François Cerruti (pen name **François Martin**) evaded the draft and supported Algerian independence. After 1962, he worked in a self-managed factory and was a member of the local section of the Trotskyist Fourth International. The 1965 army putsch forced him to go to France, where he had to do his military service. While a soldier, his participation in a mutiny sent him to jail for a few months. In the 1968 general strike, he was involved in the worker radical minority, and he was later active in "libertarian communist" or "ultra-leftist" or simply communist circles.

ABOUT PM PRESS

PM Press was founded at the end of 2007 by a small collection of folks with decades of publishing, media, and organizing experience. PM Press co-conspirators have published and distributed hundreds of books, pamphlets, CDs, and DVDs. Members of PM have founded enduring book fairs, spearheaded victorious tenant organizing campaigns, and worked closely with bookstores, academic conferences, and even rock bands to deliver political and challenging ideas to all walks of life. We're old enough to know what we're doing and young enough to know what's at stake.

We seek to create radical and stimulating fiction and non-fiction books, pamphlets, T-shirts, visual and audio materials to entertain, educate, and inspire you. We aim to distribute these through every available channel with every available technology—whether that means you are seeing anarchist classics at our bookfair stalls; reading our latest vegan cookbook at the café; downloading geeky fiction e-books; or digging new music and timely videos from our website.

PM Press is always on the lookout for talented and skilled volunteers, artists, activists, and writers to work with. If you have a great idea for a project or can contribute in some way, please get in touch.

PM Press
PO Box 23912
Oakland, CA 94623
www.pmpress.org

FRIENDS OF PM PRESS

These are indisputably momentous times—the financial system is melting down globally and the Empire is stumbling. Now more than ever there is a vital need for radical ideas.

In the seven years since its founding—and on a mere shoestring—PM Press has risen to the formidable challenge of publishing and distributing knowledge and entertainment for the struggles ahead. With over 300 releases to date, we have published an impressive and stimulating array of literature, art, music, politics, and culture. Using every available medium, we've succeeded in connecting those hungry for ideas and information to those putting them into practice.

Friends of PM allows you to directly help impact, amplify, and revitalize the discourse and actions of radical writers, filmmakers, and artists. It provides us with a stable foundation from which we can build upon our early successes and provides a much-needed subsidy for the materials that can't necessarily pay their own way. You can help make that happen—and receive every new title automatically delivered to your door once a month—by joining as a Friend of PM Press. And, we'll throw in a free T-shirt when you sign up.

Here are your options:

- **$30 a month** Get all books and pamphlets plus 50% discount on all webstore purchases

- **$40 a month** Get all PM Press releases (including CDs and DVDs) plus 50% discount on all webstore purchases

- **$100 a month** Superstar—Everything plus PM merchandise, free downloads, and 50% discount on all webstore purchases

For those who can't afford $30 or more a month, we're introducing **Sustainer Rates** at $15, $10 and $5. Sustainers get a free PM Press T-shirt and a 50% discount on all purchases from our website.

Your Visa or Mastercard will be billed once a month, until you tell us to stop. Or until our efforts succeed in bringing the revolution around. Or the financial meltdown of Capital makes plastic redundant. Whichever comes first.

From Crisis to Communisation

Gilles Dauvé

ISBN: 978-1-62963-099-1
$16.95   192 pages

"Communisation" means something quite
straightforward: a revolution that starts to
change social relations immediately. It would
extend over years, decades probably, but
from Day One it would begin to do away
with wage-labour, profit, productivity, private
property, classes, States, masculine domination, etc. There would be no
"transition period" in the Marxist sense, no period when the "associated
producers" continue furthering economic growth to create the
industrial foundations of a new world. Communisation means a creative
insurrection that would bring about communism, not its preconditions.

Thus stated, it sounds simple enough. The questions are what, how, and
by whom. That is what this book is about.

Communisation is not the be-all and end-all that solves everything
and proves wrong all past critical theory. The concept was born out of
a specific period, and we can fully understand it by going back to how
people personally and collectively experienced the crises of the 1960s
and '70s. The notion is now developing in the maelstrom of a new crisis,
deeper than the Depression of the 1930s, among other reasons because
of its ecological dimension, a crisis that has the scope and magnitude of
a crisis of civilisation.

This is not a book that glorifies existing struggles as if their present
accumulation was enough to result in revolution. Radical theory is
meaningful if it addresses this question: how can proletarian resistance
to exploitation and dispossession achieve more than aggravate the
crisis? How can it reshape the world?

*"Gilles Dauvé is well-known in certain circles for his radical ideas about the
functioning of modern capitalist society. The author has had a significant
influence on both libertarian communists and anarchists."*
—Iš rankų į rankas press (Lithuania)

Voices of the Paris Commune

Edited by Mitchell Abidor

ISBN: 978-1-62963-100-4
$14.95   128 pages

The Paris Commune of 1871, the first instance
of a working-class seizure of power, has been
subject to countless interpretations; reviled by
its enemies as a murderous bacchanalia of the
unwashed while praised by supporters as an
exemplar of proletarian anarchism in action. As
both a successful model to be imitated and as a devastating failure to
be avoided. All of the interpretations are tendentious. Historians view
the working class's three-month rule through their own prism, distant
in time and space. *Voices of the Paris Commune* takes a different tack. In
this book only those who were present in the spring of 1871, who lived
through and participated in the Commune, are heard.

The Paris Commune had a vibrant press, and it is represented here by
its most important newspaper, *Le Cri du Peuple*, edited by Jules Vallès,
member of the First International. Like any legitimate government, the
Paris Commune held parliamentary sessions and issued daily printed
reports of the heated, contentious deliberations that belie any accusation
of dictatorship. Included in this collection is the transcript of the debate
in the Commune, just days before its final defeat, on the establishing of
a Committee of Public Safety and on the fate of the hostages held by the
Commune, hostages who would ultimately be killed.

Finally, *Voices of the Paris Commune* contains a selection from the inquiry
carried out twenty years after the event by the intellectual review *La
Revue Blanche*, asking participants to judge the successes and failures
of the Paris Commune. This section provides a fascinating range of
opinions of this epochal event.

*"The Paris Commune of 1871 has been the subject of much ideological debate,
often far removed from the experiences of the participants themselves. If
you really want to dig deep into what happened during those fateful weeks,
reading these eyewitness accounts is mandatory."*
—Gabriel Kuhn, editor of *All Power to the Councils! A Documentary History
of the German Revolution of 1918–1919*

*"The Paris Commune holds a place of pride in the hearts of radicals—
heroically created from the bottom up and tragically crushed by the forces
of reaction. Yet, as this collection illustrates, the lessons of the Commune, as
debated by the Communards themselves, are as enduring and vital as that
briefly liberated society was inspiring."*
—Sasha Lilley, author of *Capital and Its Discontents*

Anarchists Never Surrender: Essays, Polemics, and Correspondence on Anarchism, 1908-1938

Victor Serge

ISBN: 978-1-62963-031-1
$20.00   304 pages

Anarchists Never Surrender provides a complete picture of Victor Serge's relationship to anarchist action and doctrine. The volume contains writings going back to his teenage years in Brussels, when he was already developing a doctrine of individualist anarchism. The heart of the anthology is the key articles written during his subsequent period in Paris, when he was a writer and then an editor of the newspaper *l'anarchie*. In these articles we see the continuing development of his thought, including most crucially his point of view concerning the futility of mass action and in support of the doctrine of illegalism. All of this led, of course, to his involvement with the Bonnot Gang.

His thought slowly but most definitely evolved during the period of his imprisonment for his association with Bonnot and his comrades. The anthology includes both his correspondence with his comrade Émile Armand and articles written immediately after his release from prison, among them the key letters that signify the beginning of his break with his individualist past and that point the way to his later engagement alongside the Bolsheviks. It also includes an essential article on Nietzschean thought. This collection also includes articles that Serge wrote after he had left anarchism behind, analyzing both the history and the state of anarchism and the ways in which he hoped anarchism would leaven the harshness and dictatorial tendencies of Bolshevism.

Anarchists Never Surrender anthologizes a variety of Serge texts nowhere previously available and fleshes out the portrait of this brilliant writer and thinker, who has reached new heights of popularity and interest.

"Serge is not merely a political writer; he is also a novelist, a wonderfully lyrical writer... He is a writer young rebels desperately need whether they know it or not... He does not tell us what we should feel; instead, he makes us feel it."
—Stanley Reynolds, *New Statesman*

"I can't think of anyone else who has written about the revolutionary movement in this century with Serge's combination of moral insight and intellectual richness."
—Dwight Macdonald

All Power to the Councils!: A Documentary History of the German Revolution of 1918–1919

Edited and translated by
Gabriel Kuhn

ISBN: 978-1-60486-111-2
$26.95   344 pages

The defeat in World War I and the subsequent end of the Kaiserreich
threw Germany into turmoil. While the Social Democrats grabbed power,
radicals across the country rallied to establish a socialist society under
the slogan "All Power to the Councils!" The Spartacus League staged
an uprising in Berlin, council republics were proclaimed in Bremen and
Bavaria, and workers' revolts shook numerous German towns. The
rebellions were crushed by the Social Democratic government with the
help of right-wing militias like the notorious Free Corps. This paved the
way to a dysfunctional Weimar Republic that witnessed the rise of the
National Socialist movement.

The documentary history presented here collects manifestos, speeches,
articles, and letters from the German Revolution, introduced and
annotated by the editor. Many documents, like the anarchist Erich
Mühsam's comprehensive account of the Bavarian Council Republic, are
made available in English for the first time. The volume also includes
appendixes portraying the Red Ruhr Army that repelled the reactionary
Kapp Putsch in 1920, and the communist bandits that roamed Eastern
Germany until 1921. *All Power to the Councils!* provides a dynamic and
vivid picture of a time with long-lasting effects for world history. A time
that was both encouraging and tragic.

*"The councils of the early 20th century, as they are presented in this volume,
were autonomous organs of the working class beyond the traditional parties
and unions. They had stepped out of the hidden world of small political
groups and represented a mass movement fighting for an all-encompassing
council system."*
—Teo Panther, editor of *Alle Macht den Räten: Novemberrevolution 1918*

*"The German Revolution of 1918–1919 and the following years mark an
exceptional period in German history. This collection brings the radical
aspirations of the time alive and contains many important lessons for
contemporary scholars and activists alike."*
—Markus Bauer, Free Workers' Union, FAU-IAA